LABOUR
MIGRATION AND
EMPLOYMENT
RIGHTS

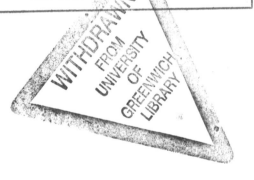

LABOUR MIGRATION AND EMPLOYMENT RIGHTS

EDITED BY BERNARD RYAN

THE INSTITUTE OF EMPLOYMENT RIGHTS
LONDON

This publication, like all publications of the Institute,
represents not the collective views of the Institute but only the views
of the authors. The responsibility of the Institute is limited to
approving its publication as worthy of consideration within the
labour movement.

Institute of Employment Rights
177 Abbeville Road, London SW4 9RL

020 7498 6919, fax 020 7498 9080
office@ier.org.uk, www.ier.org.uk

First published 2005

ISBN 0 9547562 4 X

British Library Cataloguing in Publication data
A catalogue record for this book is available from the British Library

Designed and typeset by the Institute of Employment Rights
Printed by Latimer Trend & Company Ltd, Plymouth

Contents

The contributors ix

Glossary of terms xii

Foreword : **Jon Cruddas MP and Neil Gerrard MP** xiii

Chapter 1 : **Introduction: perspectives on labour migration** 1
  1 The debate over labour migration 1
  2 The growth of labour migration 2
  3 The official approach 3
  4 An employment rights approach 5
  5 Conclusion: trade unions and labour migration 7
  Notes 8

Chapter 2 : **How immigration control fashions the labour force**
9
  1 Introduction 9
  2 The Aliens Acts of 1905-1919 10
  3 Labour migration policy after the Second World War 12
  4 The legislation of 1962 to 1971 13
  5 The unravelling of policy in the 1990s 16
  6 New Labour's managed migration 17
  7 Conclusion 20
  Notes 22

Chapter 3 : **Legal migration: the right to work in Britain** 23
  1 Introduction 23
  2 Starting-points 24
    2.1 A right to work 24
    2.2 A level playing field 25
  3 Entitlement to work in the United Kingdom 26
    3.1 Who is entitled to work? 26
      a) British citizens 26
      b) Persons with indefinite leave to remain 26
      c) Citizens of Commonwealth states with
        United Kingdom ancestry 26

d)	European Economic Area and Swiss nationals	26
e)	Turkish nationals and their families	27
f)	Overseas students	27
g)	Refugees, humanitarian protection status and discretionary leave to remain	27
h)	Spouses and children	27
3.2	The enlargement of the European Union	28
a)	The 2004 enlargement	28
b)	Bulgaria and Romania	29
3.3	The Long-term Residents Directive	30
4	Skilled employment	31
4.1	The main categories	31
a)	Work permits	31
b)	Highly Skilled Migrants Programme	31
c)	Permit-free employment	32
4.2	Reform	32
a)	The skills threshold	32
b)	Shortage occupations	33
c)	Switching into work permit employment	33
d)	Comparable treatment	34
5	Less skilled migration	34
5.1	Policy up to 2005	34
a)	Seasonal Agricultural Workers Scheme	34
b)	Sectors Based Scheme	35
5.2	Reform	35
5.3	The operation of labour migration schemes	37
6	Working holidaymakers	38
7	Horizontal issues	40
7.1	Changes of employer	40
7.2	Access to social benefits	41
a)	EEA nationals	42
b)	Non-EEA nationals	43
7.3	Settlement	44
7.4	Fees	45
7.5	Decision-making and appeals	46
8	Conclusion: the direction of reform	48
	Notes	49
Chapter 4 : Unauthorised working		51
1	Introduction	51
2	Dispelling myths	52
2.1	What is unauthorised work?	52

2.2	The interaction between immigration control and unauthorised work	53
2.3	Criminal penalties for unauthorised work	53
2.4	How many unauthorised workers are there?	54
2.5	Where do unauthorised workers come from?	54
3	Categories of unauthorised work	55
3.1	Overstayers	55
3.2	Persons with a limited entitlement to work	55
3.3	Asylum seekers working without permission	56
3.4	Clandestine entry to the United Kingdom other than by asylum seekers	56
4	Unauthorised work and labour exploitation	57
5	Evaluating government policy	60
5.1	Criteria	60
5.2	Overview of current policy	61
6	Regularisation	61
6.1	Current policy	61
6.2	Comment and recommendations	63
7	Asylum seekers' access to the labour market	66
7.1	Current policy	66
7.2	Comment and recommendations	67
8	Immigration control in the workplace	69
8.1	Current policy	69
8.2	Comment and recommendations	70
9	Trafficking for exploitation	73
9.1	Current policy	73
9.2	Comment and recommendations	74
10	Conclusion	75
	Notes	76
Chapter 5 : **Migrant workers and employment law**		79
1	Introduction	79
2	The framework of labour law	80
2.1	Unauthorised workers and labour law	80
2.2	Gangmasters and agencies	83
	a) Regulation	83
	b) Who is the employer?	85
	c) Payments	86
2.3	Coverage	87
3	Key employment rights	87
3.1	Discrimination at work	88
3.2	A written statement of terms and conditions	89

3.3	The contract of employment	90
3.4	Itemised pay statements	91
3.5	The national minimum wage	92
3.6	Deductions from wages	93
3.7	Working time	95
3.8	Health and safety	96
3.9	Dismissals and other employer decisions	97
3.10	Trade union rights	99
3.11	The freedom to change employer	100
3.12	Social security	100
3.13	Information about employment rights	101
4	Conclusion	101
	Notes	103

Chapter 6 : International agreements on labour migration 105

1	Introduction	105
2	ILO instruments	105
	2.1 Migration for Employment Convention 1949	106
	2.2 Migration for Employment Recommendation 1949	106
	2.3 Migrant Workers (Supplementary Provisions) Convention 1975	107
	2.4 Migrant Workers Recommendation 1975	109
3	Council of Europe instruments	110
	3.1 European Convention on Human Rights 1950	110
	3.2 European Convention on Social and Medical Assistance 1953	110
	3.3 European Convention on Establishment 1955	111
	3.4 European Social Charter 1961 and 1996	112
	3.5 European Convention on the Legal Status of Migrant Workers 1977	113
4	The United Nations Migrant Workers Convention	114
5	Unauthorised workers and international law	116
6	Conclusion	118
	Notes	120

Chapter 7 : Summary of main recommendations 121

The contributors

The Institute would like to thank all those who contributed to developing the ideas and recommendations contained in this publication and to making the project a success. Contributions came in a variety of forms, all of which were gratefully received and are acknowledged below:

Chair of the Working Party and Editor

Bernard Ryan	University of Kent

Contributing authors

Bernard Ryan	University of Kent *Chapters 1 and 3*
Don Flynn	Joint Council for the Welfare of Immigrants *Chapter 2*
Laura Dubinsky	Doughty Street Chambers *Chapter 4*
Sonia McKay	Working Lives Research Institute *and*
Asha Rivers	Rowley Ashworth Solicitors *Chapter 5*
Steve Gibbons	Ergon Associates *Chapter 6*

Members of the Working Party

Anneliese Baldaccini	Justice
Dick Barry	Unison *Policy & Research Officer*
Roger Bolton	BECTU *General Secretary*
Garry Brisley	TGWU *Information Officer*
Lorna Campbell	PCS *Equality Officer*
Dr Ryszard Cholewinski	University of Leicester, Centre for European Law and Integration
Nick Clark	TUC *Policy Officer* EU & International Relations Department
Collette Cork-Hurst	TGWU *Equalities National Secretary*
Pauline Doyle	TGWU *Director of Campaigns*
Professor Keith Ewing	Kings College London *President IER*
Andy Gilchrist	FBU *General Secretary*
Jonathan Green	UCATT *Research Officer*

Professor Philip James	Middlesex University Business School
Jonathan Jeffries	Trade Union Education Department, CONEL
Sarah King	GMB *Legal Officer*
Joe Marino	BFAWU *General Secretary*
Caroline Molloy	TGWU *Researcher*
Jennifer Moses	NASUWT *Principal Officer (Policy and Equality)*
David Renton	NATFHE *Equalities Services Official*
Dr Ben Rogaly	Sussex University, Department of Geography
Mary Senior	STUC *Assistant Secretary*
Maurice Sheehan	UNISON *London Regional Officer*
Dr Nicole Silverman	Centre on Migration Policy and Society (COMPAS) *Researcher*
Barry Smith	GMB *Legal Officer*
Dr Louise Sweet	Hackney Law Centre
Nidhi Trehan	Royal Society for the Encouragement of Arts, Manufactures and Commerce
Owen Tudor	TUC International Office *Head of Department*
Nicola Welchman	O H Parsons & Partners
Natalie Welsh	O H Parsons & Partners
Dr Jane Wills	Department of Geography, Queen Mary, University of London

Those who provided information on the experiences of migrant workers

Bob Blyth	Leicester City Council Citizens Advice Bureaux
Mickey Dooley	UCATT *London Regional Official*
Kate Elliot	BECTU *Coordinator* TOSCA Project
Paul Haste	TGWU Region 1/LAWA
Laurie Heselden	SERTUC *Regional Campaigns & Policy Officer*
Dr Jane Holgate	Department of Geography, Queen Mary, University of London
Daniel Holder	Animate Project, Dungannon
Catherine Howarth	TELCO
Jonathan Jeffries	ICTUR British Committee
Rita Gava	KALAYAN *Projects Officer*
Teresa Mackay	Ipswich and District Trades Council
Catherine May	Oxfam *Project Officer* UK Poverty Programme

Jennifer Moses	NASUWT *Policy and Equality Officer*
Julio Mayor	Latin American Workers' Association
Keith Puttick	Staffordshire University Law School
Margaret Sharkey	London Hazards Centre
Maurice Sheehan	UNISON *London Regional Officer*
Martin Smith	GMB London Region
Erin Van-Der-Maas	South London Citizens

Donations towards the project were received from the following unions:

AUT	Association of University Teachers
BECTU	Broadcasting, Entertainment, Cinematograph and Theatre Union
FBU	Fire Brigades Union
NATFHE	National Association of Teachers in Further and Higher Education
PCS	Public and Commercial Services Union

We would also like to thank Thompsons Solicitors for providing excellent facilities and refreshments for the meetings of the Working Party, Phelim Mac Cafferty (IER) for his administrative support and Megan Dobney (IER) for the design and production of the book.

Carolyn Jones
Director
Institute of Employment Rights

Glossary of terms

A8	Workers from the eight Central and Eastern European states that acceded to the European Union on 1 May 2004
CABs	Citizens Advice Bureaux
DTI	Department of Trade and Industry
DWP	Department of Work and Pensions
EAT	Employment Appeal Tribunal
ECHR	European Convention on Human Rights
EEA	European Economic Area
EU	European Union
HSMP	Highly Skilled Migrants Programme
ILO	International Labour Organisation
IND	Immigration & Nationality Directorate (The Home Office)
IR	Inland Revenue
NASS	National Asylum Support Service
OISC	Office of the Immigration Services Commissioner
SBS	Sectors Based Scheme
SAWS	Seasonal Agricultural Workers' Scheme
TUC	Trades Union Congress
WPUK	Work Permits UK

Foreword

Jon Cruddas MP and Neil Gerrard MP

This report provides a vital contribution to public policy making in this country when considering the controversial area of labour migration. It sets out the reasoned case for a major reform in public policy so as to improve the position of migrant workers in our economy and consequently in our society.

There is no more controversial political topic than the role and status of migrant workers in this country – witness the appalling way this territory was covered at the recent General Election.

Arguably the government has never systematically set out a clear set of principles that embrace the notion of immigration and its associated economic and social benefits. At the same time however, it has tacitly used immigrant labour to help forge its preferred flexible, north American style labour market. Authorised and unauthorised migrant labour has been central to replenishing the stock of labour needed across much of the public and private services, agriculture, construction and civil engineering. There is no reason to believe that this dependence on migrant labour in large, vital sectors of our economy will change in the foreseeable future.

Take for example, the situation in London. According to figures provided by the Office of National Statistics for the period 1992-2003, the annual inflows of international migrants into London more than doubled from under 100,000 to roughly 200,000 per year. We can assume that a large majority of those who are working illegally are resident in the capital. The government has recently estimated that these number up to 570,000 in total although this does not include dependents. In short the dynamic at work in terms of population inflows into London is extraordinary but remains unquantifiable in terms of the real levels of migration, economic activity and total population. There is no reason to suppose that the vast majority of these people will remain long term in the United Kingdom, or that the trends in migration will go into reverse.

In contrast to these economic realities, the gearing of the electoral system pushes politicians into dangerous territory when considering race and migration. The preferences and prejudices of the swing voter in the swing constituency retain disproportionate traction in our political system. As such, the modern politician seeks to neutralise – or triangulate around – difficult political terrain. There is no better example of this than the debate around migrant labour.

Yet it is through this process of triangulation that we actually collude in the demonisation of the migrant and re-inforce the isolation and vulnerability of these workers as the political landscape moves further and further to the right.

At work many feel that their terms and conditions are under threat from cheap migrant labour. In terms of their relative position in the workplace many see the role of migrant labour as a central determinant in their own relative economic impoverishment. This, in turn, remains unchallenged in most of the political debate on the labour market whilst the media and much of the political classes collude in the demonisation of the migrant.

On top of this, those communities that are accommodating the new migrant communities are often the least equipped to do so – often they themselves have the most limited opportunities for economic and social mobility.

It is this combination – the gearing of the political system on the one hand, and the economic strategy deployed by the State on the other – that creates such fertile ground for the far right.

To date, the debate around migrant labour has been fundamentally dishonest in that it has tended to discuss the issue through a focus on the relative strength of the government's immigration policy, rather than the actual material conditions experienced by the migrant worker and questions of their exploitation and issues of labour law.

Because of this – fuelled of course by the press – debate is characterised by a muscular bidding war in terms of who is tougher on immigrants. Yet these self same immigrants – both authorised and unauthorised – are the economic backbone of government labour market and public services policies. It is this fundamental rupture between the politics and the economics of migrant labour that this report seeks to confront.

This is achieved by going back to fundamental principles in terms of a framework that starts with the stated objective of respecting the rights and interests of all workers.

This framework can be contrasted with the two dominant approaches to labour migration adopted by the main political parties. This report looks at both the 'restrictionist' perspective – driven by the desire to limit the number of migrants – and the 'instrumental' perspective – looking at migration in terms of what it can offer Britain.

Both perspectives create serious labour market distortions that can only be overcome with the 'employment rights' approach developed in this report. In so doing this report alters our perspective away from seeing migrant labour issues as issues of immigration policy and toward a rights-based approach in terms of the operation of the labour market. Through the development of this approach we can then look at the consequential effects of migrant employment on the terms and conditions of other workers and in so doing materially confront some of the reasons for the hostility to migrant labour.

The report itself locates its public policy proposals within consideration of the political economy of migration in relation to the demands of the labour market. It then considers both authorised and unauthorised migration and proposes significant areas for reform both in the treatment of migrant workers and the regularisation of unauthorised workers. This analysis is then developed to cover the more general welfare of migrants both in terms of a domestic and an international framework of rights.

There are some recent initiatives that go with the grain of this report. The tragic death of at least 21 cockle-pickers on Morecambe Bay exposed the modern day exploitation and death of migrant workers and partly accounted for the passage of the Gangmasters Licensing Act of 2004. For the purposes of employment law in certain sectors this regularised the status of unauthorised migrant workers.

The effect of EU enlargement has in practice led to the regularisation of many thousands of workers resident in Britain before 1 May 2004.

The publication of the recent Immigration, Asylum and Nationality Bill reconsiders offences related to the employment of unauthorised workers. Although this Bill fails to regularise the status of unauthorised migrant workers in the way proposed in this report, it does allow a space to consider these issues of public policy and employment law over the next year.

These initiatives might well help in beginning to alter the terms of debate around race and migration in this country – arguably the greatest single failure of the New Labour government since 1997.

The contributions in the report provide a robust policy agenda for any government which seeks to confront the modern day to day realities of migrant worker exploitation. Moreover, it provides the building blocks to refashion the whole debate around race and migration in the country. As such, the Institute of Employment Rights has done a great service to public policy making in this country and we urge everyone across the labour movement to organise around these policies and their implementation.

Jon Cruddas
Labour MP for Dagenham

Neil Gerrard
Labour MP for Walthamstow

Chapter 1

Introduction: perspectives on labour migration

1 The debate over labour migration

Policy on labour migration has been a recurrent source of political controversy in the United Kingdom in recent years. The employment of asylum applicants, the opening of the labour market to nationals of EU accession states, the possibility of an amnesty for unauthorised workers, and the penalties on employers who employ such workers, have been among the more prominent subjects of political disagreement. The run up to the 2005 election also saw debate over the approach to admission for employment, with the government proposing a complex points system in its 'five year strategy' in February 2005, while the Conservatives countered with a proposal for an annual quota on admission for employment.

This ongoing debate on labour migration takes place in the shadow of the Morecambe Bay tragedy of February 2004, when at least 21 Chinese migrant cockle-pickers were drowned by incoming tides. Their deaths were shocking proof that the combination of gangmasters and unauthorised work can lead to employment which is highly exploitative and dangerous. The short-term result of the tragedy was to ensure the passage of what became the Gangmasters Licensing Act 2004. When that Act comes fully into force, probably in 2006, it will provide a licensing system which ensures the legality of gangmasters' practices in agriculture, the gathering of shellfish, and in related processing activities.

The Morecambe Bay tragedy also raised a more general set of questions about the terms in which the debate on immigration is conducted. It made manifest the artificiality of treating the status of migrant workers as a matter of immigration policy and enforcement, without regard to the employment conditions faced by migrant workers, or to respect for employment law. Tony Woodley expressed the response of many, within trade unions and beyond, in his article in *The Guardian* two days after the tragedy:

> "The rightwing response can be predicted. They will ask why these workers were in the country, not why they were working – almost certainly for very little – in such dangerous circumstances, and for whom. This is not a migration issue. It is an exploitation issue."[1]

That call to take seriously the employment aspects of labour migration is taken up in this report. What we offer is an analysis of policy on labour migration which takes as its starting-point the principle of respect for the rights and interests of all workers.

2 The growth of labour migration

Any analysis of policy on labour migration must start from the significant growth in legal labour migration to the United Kingdom in recent years. The main elements of that increase are the following:

- Favourable decisions on work permit applications (including extensions) rose from 54,050 in 1997 to 154,645 in 2003.[2]
- Permanent settlement is of significance to migrant workers because it carries with it an unrestricted right of employment. Successful applications for permanent settlement arising out of employment increased from 9,910 in 1997 to 29,600 in 2003.[3]
- Quotas for lower-skilled migration have increased sharply. Whereas in 1996, the only such quota was the 5,500 places on the seasonal agricultural workers' scheme ('SAWS'), in 2003-2004 there was a combined total of 45,000 places, made up of 25,000 on SAWS and 20,000 on the sectors-based scheme (established in May 2003).
- After eight Central and Eastern European states (known as the 'A8') acceded to the EU on 1 May 2004, 193,000 of their nationals registered as employed in the United Kingdom in the eleven months up to the end of March 2005.[4]

The phenomenon of increased labour migration cannot be reduced to a single cause. It is presumably linked to the greater ease of international travel and communication. The more benign policy environment since Labour came to power in 1997 is also a factor, but itself leads to the question, why has policy changed? In our assessment, the key explanation for both the growth in labour migration, and the changes in policy to allow it, is unmet demand for labour.

There have been shortages of skilled workers, in both private and public sectors, which have necessitated the reform of the work permit system. At the same time, in an environment of low unemployment, British resident workers have been reluctant to undertake unattractive, lower-paid work. That has led to the widening of quota schemes for such work, the opening of the British labour market to A8 nationals, and quite probably – if widespread anecdotal evidence is to be believed – an increase in unauthorised working.

The underlying demographic position is also significant. In the United Kingdom, as in every other country in the European Union, in the absence of immigration, the trend would be for the population to decline. Demographers use the concept of the 'total fertility rate', which is the number of children a woman is expected to have over a lifetime, as one measure of population trends. It is accepted that in developed countries the 'replacement fertility' rate is roughly 2.1 children per adult woman. In the United Kingdom, however, the total fertility rate is currently estimated at 1.7 children per woman.[5] What this implies is that the pressure for inward labour migration is not simply a cyclical phenomenon, varying with economic conditions and the level of unemployment. It also has a significant structural dimension, linked to the common experience of decreasing rates of childbirth in developed economies.

3 The official approach

Official thinking on labour migration has two aspects. In part, it has been based on a restrictionist logic, in that it is focused on the limiting of the numbers of migrants coming to the United Kingdom. An approach of that kind was evidenced in the policy outlined in the 2005 Conservative manifesto, to "set an overall annual limit on the numbers coming to Britain, including a fixed quota for the number of asylum seekers we accept".[6] Restrictionist thinking can however also be seen in the current government's unwillingness to provide a framework for lower-skilled migration from outside the European Union (see chapter three), and in its refusal to contemplate the regularisation of unauthorised workers (see chapter four).

There are several reasons to doubt the persuasiveness of a restrictionist outlook as a guide to public policy over labour migration. The evidence of recent policies on legal labour migration suggests that such an approach is inconsistent with the scale of inward migration required in the British labour market. In such a context, restrictions to legal migration are likely to be inconsistent with even a minimal understanding of migrants' right to work (see chapter three). The limiting of options for legal migration also opens the door to unauthorised working, which is a situation to be avoided if at all possible (see chapter four).

The lack of purchase of a restrictionist policy on current labour market conditions is the reason why it is not the dominant official perspective on immigration. Instead, official thinking is characterised by its instrumentalism. That perspective was captured precisely in the title of the document which outlined the government's five-year strategy on immigration in February 2005: 'making migration work for Britain'.[7] Within this approach, the central question – indeed, often the only one – is whether the admission of immigrants, and the terms of their treatment once admitted, maximise the advantage to Britain. Instrumentalism is the thread which links the main elements of current policy on labour migration. It explains for example the nuances of policy on legal migration which we discuss in chapter three: the favouring of highly skilled migrants, the restrictions on work permit employees, the careful management of less-skilled migration, and the general refusal to confer entitlements to social benefits. An instrumental approach also helps explain the punitive regime aimed at unauthorised workers, which we discuss in chapter four. If unauthorised work is occurring in the labour market, such a regime tends to create a highly-compliant, ultra-low-cost segment within the workforce.

A further dimension to the instrumentalism of current policy concerns the wider effects of labour migration within the labour market. In the public sector for example the inward migration of skilled workers allows Britain to meet serious recruitment gaps. As the Prime Minister put it in relation to the health service in his foreword to the 'five year strategy':

"Our vital public services depend upon skilled staff from overseas. Far from being a burden on these services, our expanding NHS, for example, would have difficulty meeting the needs of patients without foreign-born nurses and doctors."[8]

Translated, what this means is acceptance that the under-provision of certain kinds of training, and the worsening of public sector employment conditions relative to those in other occupations, are to be compensated for by labour migration. Meanwhile, the cost of educating those workers, and the consequences of their departure, are borne elsewhere, often by less developed countries.

More generally, the rise of inward migration in recent years has been associated with increased labour market competition, principally in lower paid sectors.[9] That in turn has led to downward pressure on wages and inflation, as the Governor of the Bank of England, Mervyn King has frequently remarked.[10] Increased labour market competition has also been associated with reduced costs and higher profits for labour-using businesses. The growth in profits by large supermarkets is among the more visible consequences of that process of pressure on costs.[11]

This instrumentalised approach to labour migration is open to criticism on two grounds. One problem is that, within such a mind-set, labour comes to be treated as if it were a commodity to be traded on the world market like any other, to be purchased when and if required, and always on the best possible terms. The problem, as has often been observed, is that labour in the abstract cannot be separated from the human beings in which it is embodied. Where policy does not start from the real position of migrant workers, it necessarily tends to disregard both their entitlements and their interests. The immediate consequence is to open the door to exploitative treatment by employers, and in particular, the refusal to honour contractual commitments, the failure to pay the going rate for the job, and the denial of employment rights. In the longer-term, the risk is of a failure of public policy to match the reality it is intended to govern. Migrants have their own circumstances and aspirations, and therefore retain the capacity to make choices which disrupt the best laid plans of policy-makers.

The second problem with an instrumental approach is its tendency to underestimate the interest of others in the labour market in ensuring the fair and equal treatment of migrants, whether in immigration matters or in the employment sphere. While competitive pressures because of the presence of migrant workers are most obviously a danger with unauthorised working, such labour market imbalances can also arise from the limits to the entitlement of legal migrant workers. The achievement of a level playing field in a given labour market, both between workers and between their employers, remains the key function of trade unions and of employment law. In a well-ordered labour market, public policy with respect to labour migration would aim to ensure such a level playing field, so as to avoid the damaging social consequences of unrestricted competition.

4 An employment rights approach

In moving beyond the current instrumental thinking about labour migration, this report adopts what is in essence an employment rights approach. That perspective is applied in two directions. On the one hand, employment rights thinking is brought to bear on immigration law questions, to do with the admission and treatment of migrants. On the other, the report re-examines employment law in the light of contemporary experience with labour migration.

The report is arranged so as to provide a detailed elaboration of an employment rights approach to current policy. By way of background to that exercise, chapter two provides an outline of the development of immigration policy in general, and of policy on labour migration in particular, since modern immigration control began in the United Kingdom with the Aliens Act 1905. It shows how, throughout the past century, policy-makers have sought to reconcile employer demand for migrant labour with the achievement of control both over immigration and over migrants. The current pressures towards inward labour migration are perhaps more intense than in most previous periods, while the ambition to rely on advanced technology to achieve effective control is a novelty. Nevertheless, the underlying dynamic is the same, with migrant workers tolerated, yet subject to significant restrictions, both before and after admission.

Chapters three and four address immigration law and policy in so far as these concern employment. In chapter three, the focus is on *legal* migration, including policies concerning admission – ie. the right to enter and stay on the territory – and the related issue of whether and to what extent certain categories of person have permission to take employment. Our main focus is on the implications of a 'right to work' for immigration policy and on the danger that limits to migrant workers' entitlements are inconsistent with a level playing field in the labour market. Policy on *unauthorised* workers – that is, persons present in the United Kingdom and lacking a right to work – is then examined in chapter four. The discussion there includes coverage of two important current issues: the possible regularisation of unauthorised workers, and the enforcement of immigration law at the workplace.

The report's review of labour law in the light of labour migration is set out in chapter five. A number of general questions to do with the structuring of the labour market are addressed first: the application of the doctrine of illegality to unauthorised workers, the legal regime governing agencies and gangmasters, and the limits to the coverage of employment law. That chapter then provides a detailed examination of the most important rights within employment law in the context of labour migration. It identifies possible reforms of labour law which are desirable in order to reflect certain specificities in the position of migrant workers. It also engages in a more fundamental review of employment law, simply because many of the problems associated with migrant workers are ultimately to do with the weakness of labour market regulation in general. Migrant workers are simply making visible the inadequacy of labour law for workers in general, particularly in lower-paid sectors or occupations.

Chapter six then provides a review of international action in relation to labour migration. It examines the state of play as regards international law on the treatment of migrant workers. It makes recommendations both as regards ratification of international agreements by the United Kingdom, and for the review and reform of policy in the light of international principles.

5 Conclusion: trade unions and labour migration

The objective of this report is to make a case for reform of public policy on labour migration. Its proposals deal with current issues in the field, while setting out our view of the elements of a desirable framework in the longer-term. Given its content, our hope is that the report will be of wide interest, including to policy-makers and to other organisations and individuals concerned to improve the status and position of migrant workers.

The report is addressed in particular to those within the labour movement. Trade unions have often been caricatured as labour protectionists, concerned only to keep migrants out of the labour market, in order to protect incumbent native workers. Whatever grain of truth that portrayal may once have had, it is at odds with the extensive current activity within trade unions aimed at the protection of migrant workers. There is widespread recognition within unions that migrant workers are and will remain a fact of economic life in the United Kingdom, and that the focus should be on ensuring their fair and equal treatment. That approach has obvious implications for union organisation: what this report shows is that it also implies an extensive agenda of reform of both immigration policy and employment law.

Notes

1 'The underbelly of globalisation: The Chinese workers who died were victims of cowboy capitalism', *The Guardian*, 7 February 2004.

2 Home Office, Statistical Bulletin 11/02, Table 1.5 and Statistical Bulletin 12/04, Table 1.4.

3 Home Office, Statistical Bulletin 11/02, Table 3.1 and Statistical Bulletin 12/04, Table 3.1.

4 Home Office and other departments, *Accession Monitoring Report May 2004-March 2005* (May 2005).

5 See D Pearce and F Bovagnet, 'The Demographic Situation in the European Union', *Population Trends,* Spring 2005, pp 7-15.

6 *Conservative Manifesto* 2005, p 19.

7 Home Office, *Controlling our Borders: making migration work for Britain* (February 2005).

8 Ibid, p 5.

9 See N Clark, 'A Level Playing Field for Workers', paper given at the Institute of Employment Rights conference on 'Labour Migration and Employment Rights', 14 June 2005.

10 For example, in a speech given in Bradford in June 2005: 'Migrants hold down inflation says governor', *The Guardian* 14 June 2005.

11 On migrant labour and supermarkets in Britain, see F Lawrence, *Not on the Label: what really goes into the food on your plate* (London: Penguin, 2004), Ch 2.

Chapter 2

How immigration control fashions the labour force

1 Introduction

The subordinate position of migrants in the labour force has a long history in Britain. In the 1840s, Friedrich Engels gave a famous description of the place of Irish migrants in the industrial towns and cities of England and Scotland:

"It has been calculated that more than a million have already immigrated, and not far from fifty thousand still come every year, nearly all of whom enter the industrial districts, especially the great cities, and there form the lowest class of the population... These people having grown up almost without civilisation, accustomed from youth to every sort of privation, rough, intemperate, and improvident, bring all their brutal habits with them among a class of the English population which has, in truth, little inducement to cultivate education and morality."[1]

This chapter looks at the way the relationship between immigration and employment has been expressed at different points in time in Britain. It addresses the relationship between the demand for migrant labour and the character of the immigration management or control policies which the state has adopted in different periods. What it shows is that, while immigration policies have been shaped by market conditions, they have been used not only to secure the supply of workers needed by employers, but also as far as possible to ensure their subordinate status within the workforce.

The argument is developed through an examination of the key periods of the development of labour migration policy in the United

Kingdom: the early twentieth century, the period immediately after the Second World War, the restriction of Commonwealth migration after 1962, and the 'managed migration' policy of New Labour governments since 1997.

2 The Aliens Acts of 1905-1919

Throughout the nineteenth century, the principle of the free movement of people was accepted by the political elite in Britain. While various attempts were made to introduce anti-alien bills, all were defeated, with large majorities of both Liberals and Conservatives voting against. The understanding of the time was that labour migration was a necessary concomitant of a successful trading economy. The interests of the British state in maintaining a global empire discouraged the view that movement across national borders should be restricted. The result was that, between 1800 and 1900, London was home to many of the world's political refugees, including figures such as Marx and Kropotkin. Not a single person was deported from Britain throughout that century as an unwanted economic or political migrant.

Policy began to change after the 1860s, when the Reform Acts introduced elements of democracy into parliamentary government. Prior to this time, the dominance of the *laissez faire* approach to social and economic policy had meant that immigrants were left to take their chances in the totally unregulated labour markets of the newly industrialised cities. The rise of working class resistance to the squalor which ensued began to shape the new 'national' policies of the political factions in the emerging democracy of the late nineteenth century.

Against that background, the response of the working class electorate to Jewish migration from Eastern Europe at the turn of the century was a key event. In 1901, the British Brothers League was formed with the support of the Conservative Party in East London. This was significant in that it demonstrated that anti-immigration politics could be used to reinforce the grip of nationalist ideology over important sections of the working class. It was the League's agitation which led to the introduction of the Aliens Act in 1905, which was directed at the poorest section of Jewish immigrants arriving at United Kingdom ports. The 1905 Act applied to ships with 20 or more passengers travelling in steerage class. Those persons were able to land at a United Kingdom port only with the permission of a newly created force of immigration officials. Permission was to be refused if a passenger was deemed 'undesirable', which expressly included those

who lacked the means to "decently support" themselves and their dependants.

Because of its limited scope, the practical consequences of the 1905 Act were not extensive. In 1906, for example, 935 immigrants were denied entry; but over half of the subsequent 800 appeals were successful.[2] The more important effect of the Act lay in its contribution to the emergence of 'anti-alienism' in British society, the forerunner to what later in the century was manifested as racism.[3]

In political terms, the significance of the 1905 Act was also that for the first time it breached the principle of free movement into the United Kingdom. That precedent was followed upon the outbreak of the First World War by the Aliens (Restriction) Act 1914, which allowed restriction on the movement of aliens as long as Britain was at war, or there was a situation of "imminent national danger" or "great emergency". Crucially, the Aliens Restriction (Amendment) Act 1919 maintained these powers beyond the end of the war, while removing the precondition of a threat to the state which had been set out in 1914. That in turn was the basis of the possibility, set out in the Aliens Order 1920, to require a work permit as a condition of admission for employment. The era of generalised immigration control had begun.

The decades after the First World War combined economic dislocation with political instability across Europe. Within the United Kingdom the perception that competition existed between native British workers and those arriving as migrants and refugees grew. Irish workers, the largest component of the economic immigrant group, experienced the growth of a politically-organised opposition to their presence. 'No Irish' signs were commonly affixed to advertised job vacancies in the Midlands and in regions of Scotland, and in Liverpool anti-Irish political parties obtained a substantial foothold amongst local electorates.[4]

Other immigrant groups during the inter-war years straddled the categories of refugees and migrant workers.[5] Whilst some sections of British society rallied to support refugees from Nazism, action was also taken to protect native workers in areas of the labour market. The British Medical Association secured an agreement with the Home Office in 1938 to limit the admission of refugee doctors from Germany and Austria and similar levels of opposition amongst other professional groups, including architects and academics. The Secretary of State was able to make use of powers granted by the 1919 Act to limit the admission of aliens and their participation in the labour market.

3 Labour migration policy after the Second World War

The next important period for the development of policy came after the Second World War, as the European economies commenced a period of growth under the impetus of Keynesian-inspired managed capitalism. Significant labour shortages encouraged most European countries to consider the facilitation of migration as a policy option. In most continental countries, this policy led to 'guestworker' schemes. These schemes were characterised by the central role of state authorities in organising all aspects of labour migration, from overseas selection of candidates, their direction to particular regions and industries, and the terms and conditions of their employment. Guestworker schemes were intended to be for temporary periods, with the enforcement of return abroad when the term of employment was completed.

The United Kingdom authorities experimented with a similar arrangement, the European Voluntary Worker Scheme. Between 1946 and 1950 the EVWS recruited around 180,000 Polish, Austrian, German and Baltic state nationals to work in what were termed 'under-manned industries'. These workers were subject to strict direction, working in specific industries and services, and limited in their movement outside the area where they had been sent to work. The EVWS did not prove well-suited to British conditions, however, and fell into disuse after a few years of operation. It was difficult to recruit workers to the scheme – state planners had originally envisaged 800,000 workers – and it was contrary to the *laissez-faire* principles on which the British labour market was based.[6]

There was nevertheless a readily available alternative to the highly organised EVWS. This was direct recruitment by employers of workers from Commonwealth states and the remaining colonies, particularly from the Caribbean region. Legally, such persons were 'British subjects', rather than aliens, and as such were not covered by the immigration controls which had their origins in the 1919 Act. There was a steady growth of arrivals from the Caribbean through the 1950s, from around 2,000 a year prior to 1954, to 10,000 in 1954, and between 20,000 and 27,000 a year between 1955 and 1957. By 1958 there were over 100,000 migrant workers from the Caribbean in the United Kingdom.[7]

Studies from this period have shown that overt racism – limiting access on the part of these workers to particular types of job, in certain areas – operated as the principal mechanism for controlling the Caribbean migrants. A report by Political and Economic Planning (the forerunner of the Policy Studies Institute) published in 1967 detailed the extent of racial discrimination in British industry.[8] Extensive discrimination on the part of employers ensured that immigrants moved within restricted sectors and job categories. To quote from the report:

"It is fair to say that coloured immigrants were often employed only in one type of job as regards remuneration, level of skill and interest, dirtiness and heaviness, and hours of work or type of shift; and where this was true it was the most menial and unattractive type of job, for which it has been impossible to attract white labour."[9]

Racism operated as a double-edged sword, however, in that it gave rise to unsustainable levels of discrimination and racial violence, and promoted a culture of entrenched hostility to the newly arrived. The 1958 Notting Hill riots – occasioned by friction between 'teddy boy' white youths and Caribbean residents of the West London neighbourhood – led to questioning of the consensus that British society would accept immigrants. The riots coincided with the first period of curtailment of post-war economic growth – that too encouraged some to question the idea that the economy could absorb all new immigrants. The way was now open for a wider discussion on measures to limit black immigration to the United Kingdom.

4 The legislation of 1962 to 1971

The first legislative result of the new political climate was the Commonwealth Immigrants Act 1962. That Act, introduced by the then Conservative government, imposed controls for the first time on the movement to the United Kingdom of Commonwealth and colonial citizens. A system of work vouchers, categorised into 'A', 'B' and 'C', distinguished migrant workers into those responding to specific offers of employment (A vouchers), those with skills (B vouchers), and unskilled labourers without offers of employment (C vouchers). The majority of Caribbean workers fell into the C voucher category, on which severe restrictions were imposed. Out of a total of 40,000 C vouchers issued up to 1965, only 4,000 were granted to Caribbean workers, with most of the rest (75 per cent) going to migrants from India and Pakistan.[10]

The 1962 Commonwealth Immigrants Act had been opposed by Hugh Gaitskell and the leadership of the Labour Party, on the grounds that a *laissez-faire* approach was preferable in regulating the volume of migration. This position was not sustained for long once the Labour Party came into government under Harold Wilson in 1964. Wilson's approach was for the restriction of the numbers entering, while promoting the integration of those already in Britain through race equality measures as a *quid pro quo*. This dual approach placed the principle that the limitation of numbers was essential to maintenance of 'good race relations' at the heart of the British system of immigration control, and so established the paradigm of 'firm but fair' control which has remained in place to the present day.

The 1962 Act was not conspicuously successful as a framework for managing immigration control. News of the proposals triggered an inflow of new entrants as people sought to beat the closing of the door. As many Caribbean migrants entered during the eighteen months prior to the Act coming into force in 1964 as had come during the previous six years.[11] In the face of these developments the voucher scheme fell into disarray almost from its inception. In a White Paper in 1965 the Labour government announced that C category vouchers would be discontinued. The numbers issued in the A and B categories were also sharply reduced after 1965. A limit of 8,500 was mandated for the A and B categories, which then dropped to 5,000 in 1968. The B voucher increasingly became a scheme for the recruitment of medical doctors, with 71 per cent being issued for this purpose in 1968, mainly to Indian and Pakistani nationals.[12] Even so, the voucher scheme did not prove effective in limiting the admission of migrants. Substantial groups remained outside effective control after the 1962 Act came into force: for example, a Home Office study showed that, of those who migrated in 1968, 51 per cent of Caribbean migrants and 41 per cent of Indians and Pakistanis arriving in 1968 came to join a relative who had been admitted before 1963.[13]

The 1962 Act also added impetus to what has been described as the "politicisation of black immigration".[14] The extent of this development was seen in the general election of 1964, when Patrick Gordon Walker, Labour's Shadow Foreign Secretary and a prominent critic of the 1962 Act, was defeated in a the West Midlands constituency of Smethwick in a campaign marked by explicit racism.[15] In 1967, non-white immigration again became a key political issue, as a result of the arrival of British Asians from Kenya, who were prompted to leave that country because of mounting discrimination. The agitation commenced by Enoch Powell and the popular media panicked the Labour government and led to the introduction of the Commonwealth Immigrants Act 1968. The invention of the concept 'patriality' in this legislation introduced a differentiation into the rights available to British citizens along lines of ethnicity. Those who had acquired their British citizenship through a connection with the United Kingdom – which group was largely, but not exclusively, white – were deemed to have the 'right of abode' and to be exempt from immigration control. Those whose British citizenship was derived from a connection with a former British colony – including the East African Asians – were made fully subject to immigration control measures.

The two Commonwealth Immigrant Acts were intensely controversial at the time, and gave rise to a great deal of criticism from liberal and other quarters. The evidently discriminatory objectives of the 1960s legislation were one reason for the overhaul of immigration law by the Conservative government elected in 1970, achieved in the Immigration Act 1971.

The 1971 Act was significant for its comprehensiveness. It brought aliens, Commonwealth citizens and 'non-patrial' United Kingdom citizens into the one scheme. In so doing it removed the lingering idea that Commonwealth status conferred a right to migrate to the United Kingdom. Family reunification, hitherto a right for all Commonwealth citizens settled in the United Kingdom, now became more complicated: immigration rules made the admission of spouses and children dependent on a range of requirements to do with the substance of the relationship and the ability to subsist without drawing on 'public funds'.

The 1971 Act therefore proclaimed a general cessation of labour migration to the United Kingdom. Nor was this conclusion contradicted by Britain's joining the European Economic Community on the same day that the 1971 Act came into effect, 1 January 1973. The British government saw little prospect of a high volume of new migration from the other Member States, and its desire to limit numbers was not compromised by joining the EEC.

Taken as a whole, the legislation of 1962, 1968 and 1971 marked the point at which the United Kingdom's need for economic migration, driven by the long period of post war reconstruction, came to an end. Faltering rates of economic growth led to a recurrence of unemployment and a curtailment of the high levels of public expenditure which had brought migrants into employment in such sectors as transport and health care. This legislation put in place a control bureaucracy equipped with the regulations and powers to bring about a foreclosing of migration, while ensuring discretion to admit persons where that appeared appropriate because of their individual circumstances. Henceforth the scope for new admissions would be limited to the skilled end of the spectrum, with the extension of the work permit scheme from aliens to Commonwealth citizens by the 1971 Act. Because the recruitment needs of employers were at the heart of the work permit scheme, it was expected that it would be sensitive to the real level of demand for migration in the labour market. This allowed some level of labour migration to continue even after the time when politicians had proclaimed that 'primary' migration had been halted.

5 The unravelling of policy in the 1990s

Immigration was removed from the priority agenda of the policy-makers for the best part of two decades after the 1971 Act. Economic migration was restricted during this period not just by the effectiveness of immigration control, but also by the flatness of demand in the labour markets. The main controversies were confined to family reunification issues, and for that reason were seldom taken up outside the communities most directly affected by restrictions.

This situation began to change decisively from the late 1980s onwards. The impetus for these developments came from two sources. The first was the effective collapse of the bipolar arrangements for the management of international relations, associated with the demise of the Soviet Union. The social and economic turbulence which came about during this time, including the outbreak of armed conflict in South East Europe, produced a flow of refugees. Their numbers was augmented by numbers fleeing from countries further afield, but similarly affected by political upheaval.

The second source came from new economic developments. Intensified competition had produced an elite sector of companies strongly orientated towards global competitiveness and needing to recruit its workforce from the talent available in international labour markets. Less prestigious parts of the service and manufacturing sectors also saw their operations affected by the pressures of globalisation. The hotel and catering services, always large-scale employers of migrants, were now critical to the needs of cities and regions aspiring to 'global' status, and so required extensive investment and low operational costs. Sectors dominated by retail giants as the purchasers of their produce – in particular, food production and processing – saw new conditions imposed on them which presumed the presence of a low cost, 'just-in-time' workforce. In the face of these various developments, British employers began to recognise that they once again required access to larger numbers of migrants.

Governments were initially slow to respond to these economic developments. Instead, the policy agenda came to be dominated by the perceived crisis in the control of refugees and asylum seekers. Already in the 1980s, the Immigration (Carriers' Liability) Act 1987 had introduced sanctions on the carriers of passengers not admitted to the United Kingdom, as a way of discouraging asylum seekers. The two pieces of legislation of the Major government – the Asylum and Immigration Appeals Act 1993, and the Asylum and Immigration Act 1996 – had as their main focus the reduction of the standards of reception extended to asylum seekers, in the belief that that would deter reduce the number of arrivals. Section 8 of the

1996 Act also adopted a restrictive approach to economic migration, by introducing fines for employers found to be employing migrants lacking permission to work.

These Acts failed however because policy-makers underestimated the degree of innovation required. Policy had to respond to the increased volume of refugees from countries in which political and social turmoil established an *a priori* case for asylum. It also had to address the nature of the new demand for labour migration across a wide range of sectors of the economy. The failure to do either of these things contributed to the sense of crisis in the immigration control system. This was the situation which the Labour government inherited upon its election in May 1997.

6 New Labour's managed migration

In its early period in government, New Labour's legislative efforts were limited to 'sorting out the mess' they considered to have been left them by their predecessors. Their first piece of legislation, the Immigration and Asylum Act 1999, was marked by a willingness to go further than the Conservatives in reducing the standards of reception for asylum seekers. That was done by imposing a regime of dispersal for accommodation, and support through cashless vouchers, upon newly arrived asylum seekers. The harshness of the latter measure provoked a backlash from the government's own supporters, with the then General Secretary of the TGWU, Bill Morris, threatening to support a critical resolution at the Labour Party conference in 2001. Payments in cash were eventually reintroduced, though at only 70 per cent of the level of income support, in April 2002.

A new Home Secretary, David Blunkett, was appointed after the 2001 General Election. He carried out a fundamental review of all aspects of immigration policy, which resulted in the February 2002 White Paper, *Secure Borders, Safe Haven – Integration with Diversity in Modern Britain.* This document deserves to be called the starting point of a new approach to immigration policy, based on New Labour's wider approach to modernisation and globalisation. The perspective on which it was based can be seen in David Blunkett's foreword:

> "Migration is an inevitable reality of the modern world and it brings significant benefits. But to ensure that we sustain the positive contribution of migration to our social well-being and economic prosperity, we need to manage it properly and build firmer foundations on which integration with diversity can be achieved."[16]

The White Paper proceeded from the view that immigration is an inescapable and necessary aspect of the contemporary world. Its analysis was that the task of a national government was to ensure that immigration was permitted to take place only insofar as it was in accordance with the interests of British business. To this end, immigration policy was seen as a fully integrated process, involving the selection of candidates for inclusion at the start of its procedures, and socialising them into the role of citizens at its conclusion. Throughout the middle range, the task of policy was to police migration streams, identifying those worthy enough to be admitted into 'settled categories', while expelling those who fell below the standards.

Within this new model, known as 'managed migration', immigration policy ceased to be conceived of as a measure intended primarily to limit the numbers entering the country. David Blunkett in particular argued on various occasions that there was no need to limit the volume of economic migrants, as long as they could demonstrate their economic usefulness.[17] The White Paper therefore developed an approach to immigration policy which saw its role as the provision to British companies and public sector employers of a tightly controlled workforce. Every aspect of admission and residence entitlements would be defined with reference to a worker's value to the economy.[18] At the top of the scale was the new 'Highly Skilled Migrant Programme', which allowed the highly qualified or high earners admission to the labour market without a job offer. The work permits scheme remained in place for other skilled workers with a job offer, but in practice work permits had by now become easier to acquire. For less skilled workers, the new 'Sectors Based Scheme' allowed admission to work in the food processing and the hospitality sector, but for only 12 months at a time.

'Managed migration' has also had other elements. It has involved the curtailment of asylum applications, since these disrupt the state's linking of admission to economic contribution. It has meant a preoccupation with the effectiveness of border control and immigration enforcement, in order to discourage asylum applications and to frustrate unauthorised entry or overstaying. It has also entailed the surveillance of migrants throughout the early stages of their residence. The scale of that task of monitoring the migrant population has required the cooption of other agencies, of which employers and welfare state services have been of foremost importance.

Parts of this wider 'managed migration' system had already been put in place by the 1999 Act, and these were added to by the Nationality, Immigration and Asylum Act 2002, the Immigration (Treatment of Claimants, etc) Act 2004, and many operational changes. Diverse aspects of immigration control and management have now been joined together in a fashion not previously attempted. Borders are policed both near to and far from the physical frontiers of the United Kingdom. The material support given to asylum seekers was limited through the requirement in section 55 of the 2002 Act that support be given only where a claim is made 'as soon as reasonably practicable'. That policy proved unworkable however in the face of the conclusion of the Court of Appeal that asylum seekers being left destitute could amount to "inhuman and degrading treatment" prohibited by Article 3 of the European Convention on Human Rights.[19] There are new techniques of surveillance and reporting, intended to make migrants visible at all stages to the immigration services. Immigration appeal rights have been removed, the appeals system overhauled, and legal aid curtailed. New limits have also been introduced to naturalisation, requiring migrants to demonstrate facility in English, while the Secretary of State has new powers to remove citizenship from persons who are classed as undesirable.

The ambition to continue to develop the 'managed migration' regime was signalled in the government's 'five year strategy' for asylum and immigration policy, published in February 2005.[20] Firmly rooted in the analysis that immigration is "vital for our economy",[21] the 'five year strategy' envisaged the continued access to the United Kingdom labour markets of large numbers of migrant workers. The criteria for granting admission will continue to be based on an assessment of their utility to British business and British employers.

The 'five year strategy' announcement acknowledged that managed migration had, hitherto, been "complex and difficult to understand".[22] To overcome the problems this causes it proposed a new, unified, points system. This would be structured around four different tiers: "highly skilled individuals/no job offer" (tier one), "skilled individuals with a job offer" (tier two), "temporary low skill schemes" (tier three), and "specialist workers, trainees and students" (tier four). It is difficult to see however how in practice a single points scheme can be as simple and transparent as the 'five year strategy' suggests. Despite claims for the simplification of procedures, the new proposal entails an ever more explicit hierarchy of entitlement based on the degree of a migrant worker's anticipated economic contribution. The 'most highly skilled categories' will be admitted under tier one arrangements "whether or not they already have a job". After admission they will be free to place themselves in whatever positions they consider most advantageous to themselves. On the other hand, tier two applicants will require the offer of employment in either an acknowledged shortage occupation, or where the employer has demonstrated difficulties in filling a skilled vacancy. The prospect of changing employment thereafter will be subject to the approval of the Home Office. A wide range of other differences across all four tiers are obscured by the government's claims that they system will operate as a 'single, simple scheme'.

The 'five year strategy' proposes to break with an important aspect of the work permit scheme by making the focus for an application for permission to work the position of the prospective migrant worker. To date work permit applications have been initiated by United Kingdom-based employers who have sought permission from Work Permits UK (the section of the Home Office dealing with managed migration) to employ a specified individual. Under the new proposal, a worker who has received an offer of employment will be considered for eligibility for admission by entry clearance officials based at United Kingdom embassies and High Commissions abroad. The danger is that this change will make the processes of considering prospective migrant workers subject to the differing visa procedures and world views of entry clearance officials across the globe. There are real grounds for concern that entry clearance officers operating in some African and Asian countries will operate more restrictive practices in respect of work permit applications than their counterparts in North America and other developed countries. That is the lesson of the differential application of the immigration rules relating to family reunification policies, which are applied far more restrictively in the case of African and Asian families.

A further innovation intended by the 'five year strategy' is that the ability of migrants to challenge the decisions of immigration officials on grounds of fairness and law will be severely limited. That has now been reflected in the Immigration, Asylum and Nationality Bill 2005, which contains provisions which will abolish the right of appeal for people in the various tiers of the single points scheme.

7 Conclusion

In the century since modern immigration control began in Britain, policy-makers have striven to control not only the rate of admission of migrants, but also the conditions governing their integration into domestic labour markets. The historical experience has however been that full control of all variables is beyond the capacity of government, while immigration policy has often produced a complex array of unintended consequences. Nevertheless, the achievement of comprehensive control is now being attempted once again, under the aegis of New Labour's policy of 'managed migration', and based on a belief that new technologies of control and surveillance will provide mechanisms and levers which have not been available hitherto. This plan is being reinforced by measures intended to bring

---

third parties further into the business of managing migration, including employers and welfare state services.

Whether such a scheme of total control really is possible depends on a wide range of factors, including the quality of the information technologies used, and the skills of the bureaucracies in planning for immigration and ensuring the enforcement of conditions. It also presumes a wide-ranging consensus on the part of the agencies providing the additional components of control. The political acceptability of control measures cannot be guaranteed either, since they are open to being regarded by many citizens as illiberal, draconian and disproportionate. 'Managed migration' may come to be a terrain for conflict and struggle in the period ahead, as sections of society define their own interests as being inimical to the control regimes envisaged by government.

Notes

1 F Engels, *The Condition of the Working-Class in England* (Moscow: Progress Publishers, 1973), p 116.

2 R Winder, *Bloody Foreigners: the story of immigration to Britain* (London: Little Brown, 2004), p 203.

3 Ibid, Ch 16.

4 C Holmes, *A Tolerant County? Immigrants, refugees and minorities in Britain* (London: Faber and Faber, 1991) pp 28-29.

5 Ibid. pp 30-31.

6 C Harris, 'British Capitalism, Migration and Relative Surplus-Value' in *Migration*, Band 1, Heft 1 (Berlin, 1987).

7 Figures from S Ruck (ed), *The West Indian Comes to England: a report prepared for the Family Welfare Association* (London: Routledge and Kegan Paul, 1960), p 51.

8 See W Daniel, *Racial Discrimination in England: based on the PEP Report* (Harmondsworth: Penguin, 1968).

9 Ibid. p 120

10 N Deakin, *Colour Citizenship and British Society* (London: Panther, 1970), p 50.

11 Ibid. p 49.

12 Ibid. p 51.

13 Ibid. p 53.

14 Z Layton-Henry, *The Politics of Immigration* (Oxford: Blackwell, 1992), p 77.

15 See P Foot, *Immigration and Race in British Politics* (Harmondsworth: Penguin, 1965).

16 Home Office, *Secure Borders, Safe Haven – integration with diversity in modern Britain* (2002), p 3.

17 See D Blunkett, 'A Return to Powellism', *The Guardian*, 24 July 2003.

18 For a detailed critique of the hierarchies implicit in managed migration, see L Morris, *The Control of Rights: the rights of workers and asylum seekers under Managed Migration* (London: Joint Council for the Welfare of Immigrants, 2004).

19 *R (Limbuela) v Secretary of State for the Home Department* [2004] QB 1440.

20 Home Office, *Controlling Our Borders: making migration work for Britain* (Cm 6472, February 2005). For a critical review of the proposals, see Joint Council for the Welfare of Immigrants, *Recognise Rights: Realise Benefits: a JCWI analysis of the Government's Five-year Plan on Immigration* (London: June 2005).

21 See Charles Clarke's Foreword to *Controlling our Borders*, p 7.

22 Ibid.

Chapter 3

Legal migration: the right to work in Britain

1 Introduction

This chapter provides a review of policy governing entitlement to work in the United Kingdom. In approaching that question, we recognise that there are valid ethical and political reasons to doubt the acceptability of restrictions on labour migration. In ethical terms, it is not clear why a right to live and work in Britain should be denied to individuals who are able to maintain themselves and their dependants through economic activity. The effect of a system of immigration control is to confer valuable economic opportunities on some groups, while denying them to others. It is only if economic opportunities are already thought to 'belong' to certain groups that such differentiation could be thought defensible. We support the ethical position that all individuals and groups should have equal recognition: within such an approach, it is hard to see how such a fundamental inequality in the allocation of opportunities could be justified.

The ethical difficulties with restrictions on labour migration are linked to negative political consequences. In practice, the conferral of an entitlement to work upon British citizens, and some others, while the majority of the world's population are denied it, is associated with a nationalist outlook. At certain times and places, the result has been outright racism, with differentiation purely on grounds of skin colour, or religion, or region of origin. The categorisations introduced by immigration restrictions also encourage divisions within the workforce, and as a result can undermine solidarity and effective action by workers and trade unions. The techniques of 'managed migration' discussed in chapter two also have the significant political effect of legitimising global inequality: that approach encourages the view that people from other countries, and particularly less developed countries, are to be valued only to the extent that financial profit may be made from them.

Despite these reservations as to the acceptability of limits to labour migration, this chapter nevertheless proceeds on the assumption that restrictions are likely to remain a feature of British policy for the foreseeable future. What the chapter shows is that, even if it accepted that limits to labour migration will remain, many criticisms can be made of current policies on admission and permission to work. The discussion also includes a response to current government policy in this area, as set out in the February 2005 'five year strategy', *Controlling our Borders: making migration work for Britain* and in related developments.[1] It will become apparent that in our view the current proposals would move policy even further from a framework which respects workers' rights.

2 Starting-points

2.1 A right to work

In evaluating policy on migration for employment, the starting-point of the chapter is the concept of a 'right to work'. The existence of such a right is now formally recognised in various treaties and declarations to which the United Kingdom is a party. Article 1(2) of the 1961 Council of Europe Social Charter states that "Everyone shall have the opportunity to earn his living in an occupation freely entered upon". Article 6(1) of the 1966 International Covenant on Economic, Social and Cultural Rights provides that "The States Parties to the present Covenant recognize the right to work, which includes the right of everyone to the opportunity to gain his living by work which he freely chooses or accepts...". Equally, Article 14(1) of the 2000 Charter of Fundamental Rights of the European Union recognises that "Everyone has the right to engage in work and to pursue a freely chosen or accepted occupation".

The notion that there is a 'right to work' has often been viewed with suspicion by those in the labour movement in Britain. That is because the right has historically appeared only when asserted by individual workers against trade unions or collective action. Probably the most famous example was in the 1974 Court of Appeal decision in *Langston v AUEW*.[2] That case concerned a non-union member in a closed shop situation, who had been suspended on full pay after a union objected to his employment, but who wished to continue to actually perform his contract. In support of the conclusion that the union was inducing a breach of the employment contract, Lord Denning relied upon the existence of a 'right' to work, which he described as "a right to have the opportunity of doing [the] work when it is there to be done".

It would be a mistake however to dismiss the concept of a right to work simply because of its use in a case such as *Langston*. In general terms, the right to work is to be understood as the principle that workers should not be subject to unreasonable restrictions on their freedom to enter and to leave employment relationships. Viewed in this way, the right to work provides a conceptual basis for a number of labour market principles which workers in Britain would expect to be applicable to them as a matter of course – including the possibility to resign, the freedom to change employer, the freedom to take a second job, and the possibility to move to other parts of the United Kingdom for the purposes of employment.

It is true that the concept of a right to work, as developed in the interpretation of international agreements and in other commentary, is not usually applied to the analysis of immigration restrictions. We would argue however that there is no logical reason to exclude immigration policies from its ambit. On the contrary, in the contemporary context, immigration policies are undoubtedly *the* major curtailment of the labour market freedom of workers. In our view, respect for the right to work implies that states should not impose unreasonable restrictions on labour migration. Moreover, once it is understood that there is a *right* to work, rather than a lesser privilege, the terms of the debate over the treatment of migrant workers are altered. It becomes much harder to justify situations in which their entitlements are less extensive than those of others workers or residents.

2.2 A level playing field

In addition to the right to work, this chapter also evaluates policy on legal migration in the light of the objective of a level playing field among workers. As was explained in chapter one of the report, we take the view that the guaranteeing of a level playing field is a fundamental labour market principle, and ought therefore to be a key objective of policy in relation to labour migration. In this context, what it requires is at least that all workers should be subject to the same entitlements in the labour market. The application of that principle to employment law is addressed in chapter five. Here, the focus is on the immigration rules and policies which place migrant workers in an inferior position.

3 Entitlement to work in the United Kingdom

3.1 Who is entitled to work?

In order to review policies on legal migration to the United Kingdom, it is first necessary to identify those categories of person who have an unrestricted entitlement to take up employment. The main categories are summarised in this section.

a) British citizens

Full British citizens have the right to live and work in the United Kingdom. This status can be acquired in various ways, including through birth in the United Kingdom, birth outside the United Kingdom to a British parent, residence as a child in the United Kingdom, and naturalisation. The detailed requirements in each case are beyond the scope of this report.

b) Persons with indefinite leave to remain

Those persons who are not British citizens may acquire a right of permanent residence, known as 'settlement' or 'indefinite leave to remain'. This possibility is for example open to family members after two years' residence in the United Kingdom, to economic migrants after four years, and to others after 10 years' lawful residence or fourteen years' residence irrespective of legality. Among other things, indefinite leave to remain confers an unrestricted right to work, and full eligibility to social benefits. (Current proposals in this area are discussed in section 7.2, below.)

c) Citizens of Commonwealth states with United Kingdom ancestry

Citizens of Commonwealth states can be admitted for employment if they meet the requirements set out in paragraph 186 of the Immigration Rules. They must show that at least one of their grandparents was born in the United Kingdom, that they are "able to work", and that they intend to "take or seek employment" in the United Kingdom.

d) European Economic Area and Swiss nationals

Under European Union law, nationals of the states of the European Economic Area ('EEA') have a right to work in the United Kingdom. The European Economic Area is a common market, based on an international agreement between the 25 EU Member States, Norway, Iceland and Liechtenstein. Swiss nationals also have a right to work in the United Kingdom, under a separate agreement on the free movement of persons between the EU and Switzerland. While Switzerland is not formally part of the EEA, it is treated as if it were an EEA state in British immigration law. The only employments from which EEA/ Swiss nationals may be excluded are core public sector jobs, such as those in the civil service, army and police.

There are special arrangements for workers from the eight Central and Eastern European states which joined the European Union on 1 May 2004. That question is considered in detail in section 3.2, below.

e) Turkish nationals and their families

EU law confers certain rights of employment on Turkish nationals and their families. Under Decision 1/80 of the EU-Turkey Association Council, Turkish nationals have an unrestricted right to take employment after four years' in the labour force in the United Kingdom.

f) Overseas students

Overseas students are given rights of employment as part of the policy of attracting them to British universities and colleges. Since 1999, overseas students have been free to work up to 20 hours a week during term-time, and have been free to take employment without restriction outside term-time. They also benefit from limited preferential treatment as regards employment after graduation (see section 4.2, below).

g) Refugees, humanitarian protection status and discretionary leave to remain

Those who are recognised as refugees currently acquire indefinite leave to remain – and therefore a right to work – once their status is conferred. In its 'five year strategy', the government proposed that refugees would only acquire indefinite leave to remain after five years in the United Kingdom.[3] While that proposal does not appear to affect the entitlement of refugees to take employment in the initial period, it is a retrograde step, since it will tend to make it harder to find permanent employment.

Some other persons who are not recognised as refugees are given the lesser statuses of humanitarian protection and discretionary leave to remain. The period for which they are admitted will depend on their particular circumstances. They too are free to take any employment.

h) Spouses and children

In general, the spouses and children of persons admitted to reside in the United Kingdom are free to take employment. This category includes in particular the spouses of British citizens, persons with indefinite leave to remain, work permit holders, and overseas students. Equally, EU law requires that the family members of

EEA/Swiss nationals who reside in the United Kingdom be free to take employment, irrespective of their nationality. In practice, this possibility is mainly of benefit to the spouse and children under 21 of the EEA/ Swiss national in question. Under EU law the family members of Turkish workers also have an unrestricted right of employment after five years' residence.

3.2 The enlargement of the European Union

a) The 2004 enlargement

The Accession Treaties which brought about the enlargement of the European Union on 1 May 2004 made special provision for the free movement of workers. The existing Member States were allowed to restrict the employment of workers from the eight Central and Eastern European states which joined the EU – the Czech Republic, Estonia, Hungary, Latvia, Lithuania, Poland, the Slovak Republic and Slovenia, together known in Britain as the 'A8'. For the first two years after accession, other Member States are free to apply what are termed 'national measures' as regards the labour market access of A8 workers. In the third, fourth and fifth years, the other Member States can continue to apply national measures, but must notify the Commission of their intention to do so. In the sixth and seventh years, Member States can again continue with national measures but only if there are "serious disturbances of its labour market or threat thereof", and again only if they notify the Commission of their intention.

Britain, Ireland and Sweden are the only three Member States which have not imposed substantive restrictions on the employment of A8 nationals. Britain has however placed procedural restrictions on their employment. A8 nationals are free to come to the United Kingdom to look for work, although they must maintain themselves while so doing. When they start a job, they are required to apply to register under the Workers' Registration Scheme within one month. They are free to take other jobs, but must again apply to register this fact within a month. There is a fee of £50 for the first registration, but no fee for subsequent registrations. By the end of March 2004, 193,000 accession state nationals had signed up under the Worker Registration Scheme.[4]

The consequence of a failure to register is that the employment relationship is not legally valid. The employer commits an offence of hiring an unauthorised worker. The employee, meanwhile, by being party to an illegal contract, is likely to be unable to enforce any contractual and statutory employment rights (see further, section two of chapter five).

In our view, the Workers' Registration Scheme should be brought to an end as soon as possible. The obligation to register, and to pay a

£50 fee, are more onerous than they at first appear, given that many A8 workers have limited English and limited familiarity with British systems of public administration. There is evidence that some A8 nationals have poor employment conditions, including wages below the statutory minimum, unauthorised deductions for accommodation and transport, and an absence of national insurance numbers. The willingness of A8 nationals to tolerate poor conditions appears to be linked to the charge for worker registration.[5] If it were thought necessary to monitor the number of A8 nationals, that could be achieved through an examination of new national insurance numbers, as has been done in Ireland.

The wide exceptions to the requirement to register are a further reason to reject the Workers' Registration Scheme. One exception is that an A8 national is not obliged to register if they are the spouse or child of an EEA/ Swiss citizen – including another A8 national – who is in the United Kingdom as a student, self-employed person or person of independent means. A second exception derives from the provision in the Accession Treaties that workers who on any date after 1 May 2004 have been "admitted to the labour market" of a Member State "for an uninterrupted period of 12 months or longer" gain unrestricted labour market access in that Member State. The effect of the family and 12-month exceptions is to introduce significant uncertainty as to which A8 nationals do and do not have an obligation to register. In our view, in such circumstances, it is absurd to retain a system of registration backed up by the sanction of illegality.

We also have specific concerns about the manner in which the 12-month exception is given effect in the 2004 Regulations. At present, the exemption does not benefit those who have had breaks in employment of more than 30 days in the period being counted. As the TUC has observed, this approach is unfair in the case of temporary workers.[6] There is also reason to doubt whether the terms of the exception are consistent with the Accession Treaties, which refer to "admission to the labour market", not actual employment. In our view, if the Workers' Registration Scheme is maintained, the 12-month rule should apply one year after a worker starts employment, provided the worker goes on to register.

b) Bulgaria and Romania

The next enlargement of the European Union is scheduled to involve the accession of Bulgaria and Romania on 1 January 2007. Under the Accession Treaties agreed with those states, an equivalent seven-year transitional arrangement will apply to the workers who are Bulgarian and Romanian nationals as currently applies to A8 nationals.

In our view, the imperative of avoiding complexity means that Bulgarian and Romanian nationals should be entitled to treatment parallel to that given to A8 nationals. At the minimum, Bulgarian and Romanian nationals should be allowed access to the labour market subject to procedural restrictions for the same transitional period as for the A8. We would however go further and suggest that Bulgarian and Romanian nationals have restrictions upon them removed at the same time as A8 nationals. It would be unnecessarily complex to attempt to stagger the process, by removing the obligation to register first from A8 nationals, but only subsequently from Bulgarian and Romanian nationals.

3.3 The Long-term Residents Directive

Directive 2003/109 on the status of long-term residents will be binding from 23 January 2006 in the 22 EU Member States other than Britain, Denmark and Ireland. The Directive elaborates two principles. The first is that non-EU citizens who have resided in a given Member State for five years should be eligible for protected long-term resident status in that State. The second principle is that long-term residents should have the right to take up residence in other participating Member States. During the negotiation of Directive 2003/109, the British government indicated its support for the first of these principles, but not the second, and therefore exercised its right to opt out of the Directive.

In our view, there are good reasons for Britain to opt in to the Long-term Residents Directive, and thereby to agree to mobility for long-term EU residents. Failure to do so deprives British employers of ready access to the labour, skills and experience of the more than 10 million non-EU citizens who reside in other EU Member States. It also arguably makes the United Kingdom less attractive as a destination for economic migrants, since they cannot acquire a right to move around the EU through residence here. It is misplaced in this context to be concerned to preserve total control over admission: by signing-up to the Directive, Britain would simply be agreeing to recognise the decision of another Member State to allow a non-EU national to reside there for five years or more.

Member State obligations under the second aspect of the Directive are anyway subject to limitations. Member States can refuse to admit long-term residents who cannot maintain themselves, or who are a threat to public order. They can also place restrictions on the access to employment of long-term residents coming from other Member States. While we would argue for restraint in the exercise of these options, they reinforce the conclusion that there is little reason for Britain to stay outside this EU-wide system.

4 Skilled employment

4.1 The main categories

a) Work permits

Where a worker does not have a right to work in the United Kingdom, because they do not fall within one of the groups discussed in section 3.1 above, it will usually be necessary for a work permit to be obtained before they can take employment. Work permits are issued to employers by Work Permits UK ('WPUK'), a branch of the Home Office. A work permit is then the basis for the worker's obtaining permission to enter and remain in the United Kingdom from the immigration authorities.

For a work permit to be issued, there must be a job offer which relates to a genuine vacancy which cannot be filled by a 'resident worker', defined as an EEA national or a person settled in the United Kingdom. In the standard case, it is necessary to demonstrate through a recruitment search that no suitably qualified or experienced resident worker is available. This requires evidence that the job has been advertised through Jobcentres, websites, newspapers or professional journals, etc. It is not however necessary to conduct a recruitment search for applications relating to designated 'shortage occupations'. As of July 2005, the list of shortage occupations included most healthcare positions, teachers, various engineering occupations, actuaries and veterinary surgeons.

As was indicated in chapter one, the number of work permits and extensions has increased sharply in recent years. Table 1 summarises the official figures for the period 1996-2003.[7]

Table 1

Year	Admissions	Extensions	Total
1996	40750	10910	51660
1997	43650	10400	54050
1998	47780	12050	59830
1999	53535	13790	67325
2000	67075	26195	93270
2001	81065	43240	124305
2002	85620	53170	138790
2003	81350	73295	154645

b) Highly Skilled Migrants Programme

The Highly Skilled Migrants Programme (HSMP), which has operated since January 2002, can be seen as an exception to the ordinary work permit system. Applications are made to WPUK, and are assessed according to a points system, with points awarded for educational attainment, previous earnings, previous employment, the degree of achievement in the field, and a partner's qualifications and experience. It is not necessary for there to be a specific job offer. Instead, a person admitted under the HSMP gains access to the labour market as a whole, and is free to engage in employment and self-employment. Between 1 January 2002 and 30 June 2004, 6363 applications to the scheme were approved.[8]

c) Permit-free employment

There are also some employments where a work permit is not required under the Immigration Rules. As of July 2005, these include: the representatives of overseas media organisations, the sole representatives of overseas firms, private servants in diplomatic households, domestic workers in private households, overseas government employees, ministers of religion and the ground staff of overseas owned airlines. In these cases, it is not necessary to apply separately for permission to take up employment, and all that is usually required is permission from the immigration authorities. In 2003, 10,305 extensions of leave to remain were granted for permit-free employments.[9] Statistics on admissions of those in permit-free employment do not however appear to be publicly available.

4.2 Reform

In its February 2005 'five year strategy', the government proposed a series of changes to policy governing migration for employment. The most general proposal was to introduce a points system for deciding who would and would not be admitted. On close examination, however, it turns out that the present categories are to be retained. The intended 'tier 1' of 'highly skilled' workers equates to the Highly Skilled Migrants Programme, where there is already a points system. The intended 'tier 2' of 'skilled' workers is in essence the current work permits system, and the distinction between shortage occupations and others is likely to be maintained. 'Tier 3' is to cover 'low skilled' schemes (discussed in section five, below), while the current permit-free employments are to be included in 'tier 4', made up of 'students and specialists'.

In contrast to the government's 're-badging' exercise,[10] and against the background of respect for the right to work, we have the following proposals for substantive changes to the rules governing skilled employment.

a) The skills threshold

At present, work permits cannot be issued for low-skill employment: the minimum requirement is that the post requires a university degree, HND qualification, or three years' experience of working at NVQ Level 3 or above. Our view is that this threshold should be lowered, or removed. If all of the other conditions have been complied with, it is not clear why lesser skills and qualifications, or indeed none at all, cannot lead to admission on a work permit. In our view, this would be a more realistic approach to meeting labour market need than the current quota-based labour migration schemes (covered in section five, below).

b) Shortage occupations

Our second proposal concerns 'shortage occupations'. In our view, it is unduly restrictive to insist on an employer-specific work permit in those occupations. Since, by definition, the inadequacy of labour supply has been recognised in those occupations, workers ought either to be permitted to take any job in that occupation, or allowed full labour market access. Anything less is to construct artificial barriers to their movement between employers. (That issue is considered more generally in section 7.1, below.)

c) Switching into work permit employment

An important practical issue in relation to work permits is the extent to which persons in other immigration categories can 'switch' into work permit status while remaining in the United Kingdom. The Immigration Rules and WPUK practice place significant restrictions upon the possibility of switching. As of December 2004, the categories of person permitted to switch into work permit employment under the Immigration Rules included the following:

- students who have graduated with a degree from a British education institution
- student nurses, postgraduate doctors and postgraduate dentists, but only in order to become nurses, doctors or dentists
- participants in the Science and Engineering Graduates Scheme, who must anyway be graduates with a degree from a British education institution
- working holidaymakers, after a minimum of one year
- participants in the Highly Skilled Migrants Programme.

Persons in the United Kingdom with other immigration statuses are not entitled to switch into work permit employment. This exclusion applies in particular to persons in permit-free employment, those on less skilled schemes, asylum applicants and temporary visitors. In addition, Home Office policy since 1 October 2004 is that switching to work permit status is not allowed outside the Rules, save in "exceptional cases" to do with the individual rather than the employment.

In our view, restrictions on switching should be removed, as they are difficult to justify, and inconsistent with respect for the right to work. If the work permit system is functioning properly, it is difficult to see why someone for whom a work permit can be obtained should be obliged to leave the country in order to apply for entry, not least because the result may be the loss of the job offer. The current restrictions on switching are especially perverse in the case of those in other employed categories such as permit-free employment and labour migration schemes. It would make more sense to allow those who are admitted to the United Kingdom in such categories to acquire a more permanent status.

d) Comparable treatment

A final observation concerns the requirements as to the employment conditions which must be met before a work permit is issued. The WPUK guidelines require that "the pay and other conditions of employment should be at least equal to those normally given to a 'resident worker' doing similar work", that minimum wage and working time obligations should be met, that PAYE and class I national insurance contributions should be paid, and that "deductions from the salary should be equivalent to those applied to resident workers". We support the inclusion of these obligations among the WPUK requirements, since they are consistent with the concept of a level playing field. Greater attention needs however to be paid to the question of enforcement. While there are structures in place for dealing with failures to comply with laws on wages, working time, taxation and national insurance, what is lacking is a clear remedy for a failure to treat work permit holders equally to other workers. This is a general question to which we return in our review of employment law in chapter five. There, we propose that discrimination by employer on grounds of immigration status should be a breach of the Race Relations Act.

5 Less skilled migration

5.1 Policy up to 2005

This section is concerned with policy on labour migration in so far as it relates to employment in lower-skilled occupations. There are two such schemes in operation at the time of writing: the seasonal agricultural workers scheme and the sectors-based scheme. In each case, applications are made to WPUK.

a) Seasonal Agricultural Workers Scheme

The Seasonal Agricultural Workers Scheme (SAWS) is a mechanism for the recruitment of workers from outside the EEA. The scheme operates on the basis of a quota, which is administered by designated operators. Those workers who participate on it must be students. The maximum duration of an employment is six months, and there is no provision for dependants to come to the United Kingdom.

The SAWS arrangements have been relaxed in some respects in recent years. As a result of changes announced in November 2002, all seasonal agricultural work is now eligible to be covered by the scheme, where previously the season was restricted to May to November, and there were limits on the agricultural work which could be done. The SAWS quota then increased progressively: having been set at 5,500 a year up to 1996, it rose to 25,000 in 2003 and 2004. In recent years, SAWS workers have tended to come from Central and Eastern Europe, including from states which joined the EU on 1 May 2004. The EU enlargement was accordingly followed by a reduction in the SAWS quota to 16250 in 2005.

b) Sectors Based Scheme

In response to labour market pressures, a quota system known as the 'sectors based scheme' (SBS) was introduced with effect from May 2003 in the food processing and hospitality sectors. The scheme is in essence an exceptional part of the work permit system. It is necessary to show evidence of a recruitment search, but there are no minimum requirements as to the skills and experience of the person being hired. An SBS permit can only be sought for workers between 18 and 30 who are outside the United Kingdom at the time of the application. The permit itself is limited to one year, and a subsequent application is allowed only after a two-month absence from the United Kingdom. There is no right of admission for dependants.

Initially, a total of 20,000 SBS permits was made available for the period from May 2003 to May 2004 (10,000 for each sector). As with SAWS, there was a reduction in the size of the SBS quota after the enlargement of the EU on 1 May 2004. The quota for the period starting on 1 June 2004 was reduced to 15,000 (9,000 for hospitality and 6,000 for food processing). It was also announced in June 2004 that no state's nationals would be allowed more than 20 per cent of the quota in a category in a given period. That rule was subsequently applied to suspend the issuing of hospitality permits to Bangladeshi nationals, and of food processing permits to Ukrainian nationals.

5.2 Reform

It was shown in chapter one that in recent years the combination of resident workers and inward migration from 'old' EEA states has been insufficient to meet demand in less skilled sectors and occupations in Britain. That was the reason for the expansion of the SAWS and the introduction of the SBS. It was also the reason that A8 workers were allowed unlimited access to the labour market from 1 May 2004.

One question now however is whether A8 workers are likely to be sufficient to meet deficiencies in labour market supply. In its February 2005 'five year strategy', the government set out its view that the availability of A8 workers left little need for other migration to the United Kingdom for less-skilled work:

"In the light of the additional labour now available from the new EU countries, we will phase out over time our current quota based schemes in the agricultural, food processing and hospitality sectors. We will take this forward in a review with the sectors concerned. Where additional needs are identified in future, we will introduce small tightly managed quota based schemes for specific shortage areas and for fixed periods only, with guarantees that migrants will leave at the end of their stay."[11]

The outcome of the review of the SBS was announced in June 2005.[12] The scheme is to continue in the food processing sector, though probably with a reduced quota, and will be the subject of a further review in 2006. In the hospitality sector, however, the scheme was to cease with effect from the end of July 2005. A review of the SAWS meanwhile has been announced for later in 2005.[13]

We doubt whether future policy on lower-skilled entry routes should be based on speculation that A8 workers will magically fill all gaps in labour supply. At present, Britain has an advantage in attracting A8 workers because it is one of only three states to have opened their labour market: as other Member States follow, at the latest by 2011, the supply of workers to Britain is likely to decrease. In the medium term, economic development in the A8 states can be expected to reduce outward migration, so that the classic pattern of limited intra-EU migration will assert itself for those states too. To the extent that A8 workers do come to the United Kingdom, the very fact that they have a free choice of occupations means that they cannot be expected to take the least rewarding of employments. Indeed, the government itself has begun to recognise the difficulty of persuading A8 workers to carry out certain kinds of work: it was precisely for that reason that it did not terminate the food processing part of the SBS in June 2005.

What is at issue here is not simply the retention of the SBS and SAWS arrangements, however. The logic of limiting provision to the agriculture, food processing and hospitality sectors has never been apparent, given that difficulties in the recruitment of less-qualified workers are unlikely to be confined by sector in that way. There are also reasons to doubt the wisdom of quotas as a technique for controlling labour migration, since they tend to place artificial limits on demand. This has recently been illustrated by a Department for Work and Pensions study of the early effects of the opening of the labour market to A8 nationals. It showed that roughly 50 per cent of them took work in agriculture and fishing, and that the result was a marked increase in the level of employment in those sectors.[14] The implication is that the established quota-based arrangements had significantly under-provided for the sectors in question.

Any failure of provision for lower-skilled employment is contrary to the individual right to work. Where there is significant unmet demand in the labour market, it is difficult to see how government policy which denies entitlement to work can be justified. Failure to provide adequate entry routes also creates the conditions for unauthorised employment. That has many negative consequences, including the exposure of workers to abuse and exploitation and the subjecting of legitimate employers and their workers to unfair competition, while the government itself loses tax and national insurance revenues.

For these reasons, our conclusion is that what is required is the elaboration of a general framework for less-skilled labour migration, applicable to all sectors, and not limited by quotas.

5.3 The operation of labour migration schemes

In addition to criticisms of the lack of provision for admission for lesser-skilled employment, we also have a number of proposals in relation to the detailed operation of those schemes. These observations apply both to the current SAWS and SBS arrangements, and to any future developments.

One area of concern is the method by which workers are recruited to labour migration schemes. The potential problems in this area were highlighted with respect to the SAWS in a TUC-commissioned report on Ukrainian workers published in 2004.[15] The organisation of SAWS solely through designated operators was found to have facilitated abuses – in particular, demands for bribes – by those who controlled access to the scheme in the countries of origin. There are similar dangers under the SBS scheme, since in practice potential applicants outside the United Kingdom are dependent on intermediaries, even if that is not a formal element of the scheme.[16] In our assessment, the solution is to create transparent mechanisms for the matching of workers and employers within labour migration schemes, based as far as possible in the United Kingdom.

The temporariness of the labour migration schemes is a second serious limitation of the current model. At present, SAWS workers can stay for a maximum of six months, and SBS workers for a maximum of twelve months, before having to leave the United Kingdom.

In our view, it is irrational to require workers on labour migration schemes to return to their own countries even when they and their employer wish them to stay. There is a related danger – as was made clear by the 2004 TUC report on Ukrainian workers[17] – that unauthorised employment will be the outcome. In our view, workers on labour migration schemes should at the very least be permitted to stay on with their current employers after the initial period of employment permission has expired.

Thirdly, we are concerned at the denial of family rights to workers on temporary labour migration schemes. This position is in contrast with the treatment of other categories of migrant worker. Under the Immigration Rules, work permit holders, those on the HSMP and those in permit-free employment can be joined by a spouse and by dependent children under 18, and a discretionary policy allows the admission of parents and adult dependent children. EEA workers meanwhile benefit from the family rights set out in EU law, which give rights of admission to the spouse, dependent parents and grandparents, and children who are under 21 or dependent. The denial of rights of family admission to SAWS and SBS workers is typical of an instrumental approach to these workers. They are treated as mere possessors of labour, with any social or family dimension to their lives simply ignored. Our view is that, at the minimum, workers on temporary labour migration schemes ought to be permitted to bring their spouse and children with them.

6 Working holidaymakers

The working holidaymaker scheme is a long-standing arrangement whereby citizens of Commonwealth states can be admitted to the United Kingdom for up to two years. The main eligibility requirements are that the individual is between 17 and 30, that they intend to leave the United Kingdom at the end of their stay, and that they are able to pay for a return or onward journey. In 2003, 46,500 persons actually entered the United Kingdom in this category.[18]

Changes to the working holidaymaker scheme which came into effect in August 2003 made it significantly less restrictive than previously. All limitations on the employment which can be undertaken were removed, whereas before working holidaymakers had not been allowed to work for more than 25 hours a week for more than 50 per cent of the stay, had not been allowed to pursue a career in Britain, and had not been allowed to take employment in sports and entertainment. It also became possible in August 2003 for a working holidaymaker to apply to switch to work permit employment after one year in the United Kingdom. The net effect of these changes was that the working holidaymaker scheme was more likely to be a route to longer-term employment to Britain.

Many of the 2003 changes were then reversed in February 2005, as part of the 'five year strategy'. The requirement that work be incidental to a holiday was re-asserted, with a prohibition on the total period of employment exceeding one year. The possibility to take employment in sport was removed. In addition, the possibility to switch into work permit employment was restricted to designated 'shortage occupations'.

One well-known problem with the working holidaymaker scheme is its bias towards the 'old' Commonwealth states, and therefore towards white applicants. An impression of this can be gauged from the 2003-2004 figures, which show that, of 59,822 successful applications worldwide, 24,996 were in Australia and New Zealand (42 per cent), 19,906 in South Africa (33 per cent), and 5,389 in North America (nine per cent). It is also the case that individual applicants in other parts of the world find it harder to succeed: in 2003-04, there was a 63 per cent refusal rate in South Asia, a 33 per cent refusal rate in Equatorial Africa, and a 28 per cent refusal rate in the West Indies/Guyana, as against a 0.7 per cent refusal rate in North America and a 0.3 per cent refusal rate in Australia and New Zealand.[19] Our view is that a way should be found to ensure that the benefits of the working holidaymaker system are genuinely available to all Commonwealth citizens on an equal basis. While there are several ways in which that result might be achieved, we take the view that part of the solution would be an annual quota per state or region.

As recently as 2002, the government set out the ambition to make the working holidaymakers scheme "as inclusive as possible".[20] The disparities within it are however likely to be exacerbated if the government carries out the proposal, announced in the 'five year strategy', that the scheme "only be available to nationals of countries with a satisfactory returns arrangement with the UK".[21] Such a condition is more likely to apply to less developed Commonwealth states, which are precisely those whose nationals currently benefit least from the scheme. For that reason, we cannot support this proposal to restrict access to the working holidaymaker scheme.

We would also highlight the lack of provision for family rights for working holidaymakers: while they can bring children under the age of five, no provision is made for spouses. It is unclear why this limitation applies, given that they may stay for two years, and may eventually switch to work permit employment. As with temporary labour migration schemes, our view is that working holidaymakers ought to be entitled to be accompanied by their spouse and any minor children.

7 Horizontal issues

Having considered the main aspects of policy on the admission of workers, this section looks at a number of cross-cutting issues which apply to various categories of labour migration.

7.1 Changes of employer

The rules on the possibility for migrant workers to change employer are of fundamental importance within the labour market. The operation of the labour market in allocating labour to where it is most useful, and the individual's right to work, each point in the direction of allowing migrant workers to change employer where they consider it advantageous to them to do so. There are also basic issues as regards fairness. The narrower a worker's options as regards a change of employer, the greater the scope for an employer to impose unfair pressure as regards performance, conditions at work, or terms of employment. This is a matter of legitimate concern not just to the individual in question, but to interested third parties such as co-workers and trade unions.

By contrast, current arrangements place significant limitations on the ability of migrant workers to change employer. In the case of work permits, permission to work is formally limited to a specific employer. It is true that in practice WPUK will issue a new work permit for a new employer, without the need for a recruitment search, provided the work to be done is within the same occupation. That possibility is however a limited one: it is not a legal entitlement and depends on the second employer's willingness to apply for a work permit. Nor does it permit a change of occupation, even though this may be important in cases where the employment relationship with a first employer has broken down. Our solution would be to allow an unlimited right to change employer and occupation after a short period, such as three months, has elapsed.

The approach taken to changes of employer within labour migration schemes requires particular consideration. At present, SAWS workers are permitted to change employer only if they remain attached to the operator with which they came to Britain. SBS permit holders are permitted to change employers provided they carry out the same occupation. The difficulty with restrictions of this kind is that workers on labour migration schemes are often the most vulnerable to employer sharp practice. Evidence of this can be found in the TUC study of Ukrainian workers cited above, which found examples of SAWS employers failing to honour their commitments under the scheme.[22] Part of the answer to the weak position of workers within labour migration schemes is to strengthen the rights of workers to change employer. Our solution would simply be to allow changes of employer within the scheme from the outset – given the short-term nature of this employment, any lesser entitlement would be insufficient to address the position of those workers.

A further issue in this context is the proposal in the 'five year strategy' that employers should become the formal sponsors of those admitted to the United Kingdom for employment. This proposal would apply to the employers of work permit holders, of those in permit-free employment, and of those on labour migration schemes. Although the full details are not clear at the time of writing, the February 2005 document made clear that sponsors would "share the responsibility of ensuring that migrants comply with the requirements attached to their leave", and that they would "be expected to... report if the migrant has left employment".[23] This proposal is likely to affect the possibility to change employer in particular, since it is hard to reconcile a position whereby employers are sponsors with the freedom of the employee to change job. In any event, potential new employers are likely to be reluctant to take on the obligations of sponsors, so that any possibility to change employer will be reduced in its effectiveness. For these reasons, we reject the proposal to place the obligations of sponsorship on employers.

7.2 Access to social benefits

Migrant workers are often portrayed as being attracted to the United Kingdom by its social welfare scheme. The reality however is quite different, since there are restrictions on eligibility which prevent migrant workers claiming non-contributory benefits – ie. those that do not depend upon a period of employment or contribution to national insurance. These benefits include in particular income-based jobseekers' allowance, child benefit, housing benefit and council tax benefit.

In our assessment, the question of access by migrant workers to non-contributory benefits is of fundamental importance. What is at issue here is the avoidance of a situation in which a worker is faced with a choice between accepting oppressive conditions at work and destitution, through lack of an income, if they refuse. This is not something which other workers in the British labour market would accept, and neither should it be permitted in a wealthy society. This is an area where the notion of a level playing field has particular relevance: other workers in a labour market should not be faced with competitive pressure because some migrant workers accept exploitative conditions in order to avoid destitution. Viewed in that light, current policy on migrant workers' access to social benefits is seriously deficient. For clarity, the cases of EEA nationals and non-EEA workers are treated separately.

a) EEA nationals

Workers from EEA countries are entitled to social benefits in two main ways. In the first place, the EU system for the co-ordination of social security systems (based on EU Regulation 1408/71) protects those who, having been covered by the social insurance system in another Member State, switch their residence to the United Kingdom. Even before they enter employment, such persons are eligible for most contributory and non-contributory benefits, including those relating to sickness, maternity, invalidity, accidents at work, unemployment and families.

The alternative for those who are not attached to the social security system of another Member State is to rely on the right of equal treatment to 'social advantages' set out in Article 7(2) of EU Regulation 1612/68. That requires that EEA migrants who cease employment in the United Kingdom can claim equality in benefits relating to unemployment. In the case of workers who are looking for work, but who have not yet taken up employment in the United Kingdom, however, EU law does not require equal treatment unless the worker has a genuine link to the British labour market.[24] Since 1994, moreover, British social welfare law has restricted non-contributory benefits to those who are 'habitually resident' in the United Kingdom or Ireland.

The desire to prevent A8 nationals from claiming social benefits led to the introduction of a further restriction with effect from 1 May 2004. The Social Security (Habitual Residence) Amendment Regulations 2004 redefined the 'habitual residence' test so that only persons with a 'right to reside' in the United Kingdom or Ireland could be treated as habitually resident and so have access to income-related benefits. At the same time, the new immigration regulations for A8 workers mean that they do not have a right of residence unless they are actually in work. The result is that A8 nationals – and only A8 nationals – who cease employment are ineligible for non-contributory benefits. The only way they can qualify is if they are exempt from the Workers' Registration Scheme, which is most likely to arise because they have met the test of 12 months on the labour market, or are the family member of an A8 national who is self-employed or a student.

Because of the importance of the principle that workers should have access to basic social benefits, we take the view that the current restrictions applicable to EEA nationals should be removed. In the first place, workers who have come to the United Kingdom in order to look for work should be entitled to social benefits while so doing. Not to do so risks creating a situation where they are forced to accept poor quality employment offers. It is precisely in order to avoid that risk that Irish workers, who have historically filled many less skilled jobs in Britain, have always been given access to social benefits from day one, and continue to be so. Now that public policy is for A8 and other EEA nationals to fill that role, it is hard to see what justification there is for excluding them from benefits while they are looking for work. The only counter-argument is the fear of so-called 'benefit tourism'. In our view, however, it is highly unlikely that workers will move countries in order to obtain what are essentially subsistence payments, and in any event, there are well-established administrative mechanisms to check on the genuineness of an individual's desire to work in the United Kingdom.

The case for A8 workers being given access to post-employment benefits is even stronger. These are workers who by definition have already worked and made an economic contribution in the United Kingdom. Their exclusion from benefits is discriminatory by comparison with British and other EEA nationals. We would add that there are anyway reasons to doubt that the new regulations are consistent with the Accession Treaties, which do not permit the postponement of the application of the right to equal treatment in social advantages set out in Article 7(2) of Regulation 1612/68. In our assessment, the gross unfairness of excluding A8 workers from post-employment benefits ought to be remedied without delay.

b) Non-EEA nationals

A migrant worker who comes from outside the EEA essentially has no entitlement to welfare benefits. All of those admitted for employment to the United Kingdom are subject to a condition that they do not have recourse to public funds. They are subsequently eligible for contributory benefits, if they have the necessary national insurance contribution record. However, under section 115 of the Immigration and Asylum Act 1999, they are a "person subject to immigration control" who is precluded from claiming non-contributory benefits. The benefits denied them include child benefit, council tax benefit, the working families tax credit, housing benefit, and job-seekers' allowance.

Here too, we take the view that it is fundamentally undesirable that migrant workers are discriminated against in access to non-contributory benefits. It is unfair on the workers themselves, given that they will have been admitted to take employment, and will have almost certainly made an economic contribution in Britain. It leaves them more vulnerable to employer pressure, because of their fear of loss of income or of eventual destitution.

7.3 Settlement

In practice, the question of the right to change employer is bound up with the acquisition of settlement, or 'indefinite leave to remain'. For migrant workers, the general principle is that, after four years, those who have been engaged in economic activity as work permit holders or in permit-free employment are entitled to obtain indefinite leave to remain. With it, they acquire rights of employment and self-employment, and full access to social benefits. After 12 months with indefinite leave to remain, they are able to apply to naturalise as a British citizen, which in turn confers rights of migration to other EEA states.

Given the importance to the individual of obtaining settlement, we are concerned by certain restrictions upon the entitlements of those with four years' economic activity. One difficulty concerns the requirement in the Immigration Rules that work permit holders and those in permit-free employment must have their employer certify that they are "still required for the employment in question". While most employers comply with this request, it is not obvious why the employer's permission should be required, not least because it may be in the employer's interest to frustrate the application for settlement. We would also point out that for self-employed categories and for the HSMP, the Immigration Rules merely require evidence that the individual has been in economic activity for the four-year period. In our view, an application for settlement should simply depend on proof that an individual is in employment at the end of the four-year period.

A second difficulty with the provision for settlement of those on work permits or in permit-free employment arises where an individual switches between categories. The general rule is that it is not possible to aggregate periods spent in different immigration categories for the purpose of a settlement application arising out of employment. An exception is made in the case of those on the HSMP, who may for example count periods of residence on a work permit, although not time spent as a student or working holidaymaker. There does not seem to be a clear reason why someone who switches into work permit employment or permit-free employment should not be allowed to count periods spent in the United Kingdom on some other basis. Provision for aggregation seems especially appropriate for temporary work or study categories from which it is possible to switch into work permit employment.

The significance of settlement to the labour market status of individuals leads us to disagree with two proposals in relation to settlement set out in the February 2005 'five year strategy'.[25] The first is that employment should lead to indefinite leave to remain only after five years' employment, rather than four at present. The second is that permit-free employment should no longer lead to settlement at all. Neither of these proposals has a clear justification within the 'five year strategy', apart from (again) a desire to "increase the economic benefit to the UK of permanent settlement". In our view, the significance of settlement for an individual's labour market position makes each of these proposals a retrograde step.

7.4 Fees

Recent years have seen the application of a new approach to charges for employment permissions and related immigration documents. The policy is to seek full cost recovery, based on the theory that the processing of applications and the issuing of documents are services provided to migrants. The 'five year strategy' was explicit that "We will continue to recover the costs of the scheme through charges on migrants, to enable us to offer the most efficient service".[26]

The result of this policy has been the introduction of onerous fees. One charge is made for what are termed "immigration employment documents" – ie. work permits, HSMP permission, SBS permits, and SAWS work cards. Having been authorised by the Nationality Immigration and Asylum Act 2002, charges for these documents came into effect on 1 April 2003. As of July 2005, the fee for the HSMP is £315, the fee for work permit and SBS applications is £153, and the fee for a SAWS application is £12. A second charge was introduced, with effect from 1 April 2004, for applications to extend the leave to remain of those on work permits, or covered by the HSMP, SBS and SAWS. Having been set initially at £121, the charge for these applications was increased to £335 with effect from April 2005. These are in addition to charges for settlement applications, which since 1 April 2005 have been set at a minimum of £335. As has been explained, settlement is of particular interest to those in employment, because it removes restrictions on their entitlement to work.

In our view, the application of the principle of full cost recovery to employment permissions and related immigration applications is inherently questionable. The checking of applications and the issuing of employment and immigration documents are not services to actual or intending migrants, but rather obligations placed upon migrants by the immigration authorities, in order that the authorities may decide who to admit or permit to stay. We are also concerned that the level of fees for employment documents and related immigration applications may be such as to deter those on lower incomes from applying. If fees are retained, they should be set at a low level, so as not to deter migration, and so as to reflect the obligatory nature of the immigration control process.

We would also question whether the current charges are consistent with respect for migrants' right to work. The content of Article 18(2) of each of the Council of Europe Social Charter 1961 and of its revised version of 1996 is instructive. These oblige contracting States, including Britain, to "reduce or abolish chancery dues and other charges payable by foreign workers or their employers". Article 18(2) prevents the application of the charges for employment permissions and for immigration employment documents to nationals of 10 Council of Europe states (Albania, Andorra, Armenia, Azerbaijan, Bulgaria, Croatia, Macedonia, Moldova, Romania and Turkey). More generally, it is evidence for the proposition that, where other conditions are met, the exercise of the right to work ought not to be obstructed by financial charges levied by state authorities.

7.5 Decision-making and appeals

At present, the decision-making process on most labour migration applications is in two parts. The first stage is the employment authorisation. Applications for work permits, the HSMP, SAWS and SBS are made to WPUK. The exceptions are that specific employment authorisation is not needed for permit-free employments or for the working holidaymaker scheme. The second stage is for the worker to obtain permission to enter the United Kingdom. For most of the categories discussed here, it is necessary to obtain pre-departure 'entry clearance' in the place where the individual is currently living. The exceptions are the holders of work permits of six months or less who are not visa nationals, and participants in the SAWS. In these cases, immigration permission can be granted at the port of entry.

The regime governing appeals – which since 4 April 2005 have been taken to the Asylum and Immigration Tribunal – is also in two parts. There is no right of appeal against the refusal of immigration employment documents – that is, work permits, SBS permits, SAWS work cards, HSMP permissions, or an extension of any of those. This is because the refusal of an employment permission does not count as an 'immigration decision' against which there is a right of appeal under section 82 of the Nationality Immigration and Asylum Act 2002. Where an immigration employment document is refused, all that is available is an administrative reconsideration by WPUK. It is however possible to appeal against the refusal of immigration permission, save that that avenue cannot be used to re-open the question of whether employment permission should have been granted. The result is that the appeal right is of most practical value for employments where such permission is not needed – ie. permit-free employment and the working holidaymaker scheme.

The 'five year strategy' includes two proposals in this area. The first is to "merge the current immigration and employer checks into a single, pre-entry check".[27] While the details of the intended arrangements remain uncertain at the time of writing, it seems likely that both aspects will be dealt with through the entry clearance process. We would question the desirability of such a step, since it would involve giving decision-making power over employment matters to non-specialist officials, and would probably lead to variability in decision-making in different posts around the world. If a single check is to be introduced, it should be carried out centrally, presumably by WPUK.

The second proposal is that even the limited current appeal rights in employment contexts should be removed, on the grounds that "the issues raised are less important" than in the case of asylum and family applications.[28] At the time of writing, this second proposal is being implemented through the Immigration Asylum and Nationality Bill 2005.

We take a quite different view of what is required in relation to appeal rights. It is a basic principle of administrative law that individuals ought to have a remedy against illegal or flawed decisions taken with respect to them by public bodies. The appeal route has significant practical advantages over judicial review, because of the greater potential cost and delay of judicial review proceedings. In addition, an appeal can revisit both the factual and legal aspects of the initial decision, and can lead to the tribunal's substituting its decision for that of the original decision-maker. Judicial review by contrast is concerned above all with the reasonableness and fairness of the decision, and usually leads only to reconsideration by the original decision-maker.

In the employment context, respect for the right to work must entail an effective remedy against negative decisions on employment permissions and on related decisions concerning admission. The formulation that these are questions which are simply "less important" seems to us to trivialise the significance of the issues which may be at stake for an individual if permission is denied them. Rather than curtailing appeal rights in this area, public policy ought to be based on the principle that here, just as in any other context, individuals are entitled to effective remedies against adverse decisions by public authorities.

8 Conclusion: the direction of reform

The proposals set out in this chapter are very different to those currently being pursued by the government. Based on the instrumental philosophy of its 'five year strategy', the government has curtailed the working holidaymaker scheme, and has begun the process of restricting lower-skilled entry, limiting the freedom to change employer, and removing appeal rights. The proposal to introduce a general points system, which on its face changes little, also has negative implications. One danger for migrants and employers is the points levels will be changeable, thereby introducing uncertainty as regards admission for employment and extensions. In the longer-term, moreover, a generalised points system may make it easier to introduce quotas on migration for employment. That is because it involves a movement away from setting down conditions which, once satisfied, give an individual an entitlement to be admitted.

The analysis set out in this chapter points in another direction. We take the view that the focus of policy initiatives should be on widening the present systems of access to the labour market. The Workers' Registration Scheme for A8 nationals should be abolished. The conditions for work permits should be relaxed. A general route of entry for lower-skilled employment should be created, and the terms of such schemes made more equitable. The principles of unrestricted access to the labour market and the related right to change employer, which are at present conferred only within the HSMP, should be available more widely. Social benefits should be available to all workers in the labour market. These are the minimum reforms which are required if the right to work of migrant workers, and the entitlement of all workers to a level playing field, are to be respected.

Notes

1 Home Office, *Controlling Our Borders: making migration work for Britain* (Cm 6472, February 2005).

2 [1974] ICR 180.

3 Home Office, *Controlling Our Borders,* p 22.

4 Home Office and other departments, *Accession Monitoring Report May 2004-March 2005* (May 2005).

5 See Trades Union Congress, *Propping up Rural and Small Town Britain: migrant workers from the New Europe* (November 2004), Ch 5, and the special report by Felicity Lawrence, 'Polish workers lost in a strange land find that work in UK does not pay', *The Guardian,* 11 January 2005.

6 TUC, *Propping Up,* p 21.

7 Home Office, Statistical Bulletin 11/99, Tables 2.3 and 2.4 and Statistical Bulletin 12/04, Table 1.4.

8 Written answer by Immigration Minister, Des Browne, House of Commons, 16 November 2004.

9 Home Office, *Control of Immigration: Statistics – United Kingdom 2003* (Cm 6363, November 2004), Table 4.1.

10 For this term, see Joint Council for the Welfare of Immigrants, *Recognise Rights: Realise Benefits: a JCWI analysis of the Government's Five-year Plan on Immigration* (London: 2005), p 4.

11 Ibid.

12 Written statement by Immigration Minister, Tony McNulty, House of Commons, 23 June 2005.

13 Written answer by Home Office Minister, Baroness Scotland, House of Lords,
7 June 2005.

14 J Portes and S French, *The Impact of Free Movement of Workers from Central and Eastern Europe on the UK Labour Market: early evidence* (June 2005), Ch 5.

15 TUC, *Gone West: Ukrainians at work in the UK* (March 2004), pp 15-18.

16 Ibid, p 26.

17 Ibid, p 25.

18 *Control of Immigration: Statistics – United Kingdom 2003,* Home Office Statistical Bulletin 12/04, Table 1.2.

19 UK Visas, *Entry Clearance Statistics 2003-2004,* pp 55-64.

20 Home Office, *Secure Borders, Safe Haven: integration with diversity in modern Britain* (Cm 5387, February 2002), p 45.

21 Home Office, *Controlling Our Borders,* p 16.

22 TUC, *Gone West,* pp 19-20.

23 Home Office, *Controlling Our Borders,* p 16.

24 This is the implication of the Court of Justice decision in *Collins,* Case C-138/02, 23 March 2004.

25 Home Office, *Controlling Our Borders,* p 22.

26 Ibid, p 16.

27 Ibid, p 17.

28 Ibid, pp 10 and 19.

Chapter 4

Unauthorised working

1 Introduction

This chapter is about migrants who require authorisation to work and are working without proper authorisation. It is instructive to begin by recalling what has been said in public debate:

"This is the modern day slave trade. Lured to Britain with little knowledge of English, illegal immigrants are forced to work 12 hours a day, six days a week, for derisory amounts of money. Health and safety regulations don't apply. They are kept outside the confines of society and beyond the reach of the law. If we had a government prepared to face up to the problem of illegal immigration into the United Kingdom then [the Chinese cocklepickers] who perished in the rising tides [at Morecambe Bay] might still be alive today. The government has both the resources and the manpower to clamp down on illegal immigrants... but instead of dealing with illegal immigration and the human suffering it leads to, the government has turned its back on it..."[1]

These extracts, taken from a *Mail on Sunday* article by David Davis, Conservative Party shadow Home Secretary, typify two trends in the debate about unauthorised working. First, there is split thinking about migrant workers who engage in unauthorised working. Unauthorised workers are vilified as criminals and parasites but simultaneously portrayed as the passive victims of extreme abuse who deserve public pity. Second, there is confusion between action against unauthorised working (the enforcement of immigration control) and action on behalf of unauthorised workers (the enforcement of labour standards and the protection of fundamental human rights).

The material in this chapter is divided into two parts. The first part of the chapter (sections 2 to 4) sets the scene. It attempts to dispel some of the confusion surrounding the topic of unauthorised work by examining how it arises, summarising relevant law, distinguishing various categories of unauthorised work and reviewing labour conditions among unauthorised workers. The second part of the chapter (sections 5 to 9) then examines present government responses to unauthorised working and makes recommendations. We argue that new emphasis must be placed on labour standards protection and the protection of fundamental human rights for unauthorised workers present in the United Kingdom.

This chapter uses the term 'unauthorised working' rather than the term 'illegal working' used by the government and press, since the latter encourages the association of unauthorised working with criminality. The European Economic and Social Committee has stated of the use of the term 'illegal' with reference to individual migrants that:

> "although it is not lawful to enter a country without the required documents and authority, those who do so are not criminals. Lumping together irregular immigration and crime... distorts the facts and breeds fear-driven and racist attitudes among the general public. Unauthorised immigrants are not criminals although their situation is not legal."[2]

The same can clearly be said of those who work without the required documents or authority.

2 Dispelling myths

2.1 What is unauthorised work?

In the public mind, unauthorised work is linked with clandestine entry to the United Kingdom for purposes of work, with the informal economy and with migration from the developing world. These associations are misleading.

Unauthorised work is *not* limited to people who enter the United Kingdom clandestinely, who never obtain permission to be in the United Kingdom, and who remain hidden in the informal economy.[3] It is a far broader phenomenon. An immigrant or an asylum seeker who has a form of permission to be in the United Kingdom which prohibits them from working at all or from doing more than a certain number of hours, or which restricts them to a particular form of work, can engage in unauthorised work if they breach those restrictions. Given the complexity of the restrictions on working in the United Kingdom, a person may (sometimes inadvertently) switch back and forth between regular and unauthorised work.

Unauthorised work is a highly amorphous phenomenon arising in many sectors of the economy. It includes the IT consultant on a work permit who has switched job without permission; the overseas student who is working too many hours at a bookshop; the asylum seeker who is working in a factory while awaiting determination of her asylum claim; the young backpacker who has overstayed his visit visa and is working as a barman; and the cocklepickers of Morecambe Bay who had arrived and were living clandestinely in the United Kingdom.

2.2 The interaction between immigration control and unauthorised work

As is set out in more detail in chapter two on the history of immigration controls, immigration legislation has developed in an *ad hoc* way to deal with new forms of immigration.

The Immigration Act 1971 sets the foundation for the present system of immigration control. In summary, 'leave' (permission) to enter the United Kingdom is not required by the following: British citizens, Commonwealth citizens who have a right of abode (ie. a right to live in and come and go freely) in the United Kingdom, and holders of passports from other countries within the European Economic Area who are exercising free movement rights.

Almost all other people are 'subject to immigration control': they require 'leave' to enter or remain in the United Kingdom. Foreign nationals may be granted leave to enter or remain in the United Kingdom for a variety of reasons – as a visitor, a student, a spouse, etc – the criteria for which are set out in the Immigration Rules. Unless a person is granted indefinite leave to remain (ie. the right to remain permanently in the United Kingdom) their leave to enter will be of limited duration. Limited forms of leave may be subject to conditions, including conditions concerning employment. For example, a person who enters the United Kingdom as a visitor (usually for six months) will normally be prohibited from working. A person who enters the United Kingdom as a student will have permission to work for only 20 hours a week during term-time, and full-time only during vacations.

As already set out above, a person who, by working, breaches the conditions of their limited leave to enter the United Kingdom, will be working without authorisation. Having breached the conditions of their limited leave to enter, they are liable to have their leave to remain revoked, and to be detained and removed.

2.3 Criminal penalties for unauthorised work

There is widespread confusion about whether a person who engages in unauthorised work is committing a criminal offence. Illegal entry to the United Kingdom, overstaying and breaching the conditions of one's leave are all summary criminal offences under section 24 of the Immigration Act 1971, punishable by up to six months' imprisonment and a fine of up to £5,000. Therefore, if someone works in breach of the conditions attached to their limited leave to enter, they commit a criminal offence. If the worker has entered illegally, or is an overstayer (someone who has stayed beyond the limited period they had permission to stay in the United Kingdom), it is the illegal entry or overstaying which constitutes the criminal offence. There is no additional criminal offence of 'illegal work'.

In practice, where a person is discovered working without permission, the result will often be that they will be placed in immigration detention (administrative, not criminal) before being administratively removed from the United Kingdom.

As is set out in more detail in section 8 of this chapter below, it is a criminal offence under section 8 of the Asylum and Immigration Act 1996, punishable by fines of up to £5,000 per employee, to employ a person who does not have a right to work in the United Kingdom or who does not have a right to do the particular form of work or hours of work they are doing. It is the employer, not the employee, who commits this criminal offence. Employers are, however, very rarely prosecuted for this offence. It is therefore employees, not employers, who bear the brunt of detection.

2.4 How many unauthorised workers are there?

There are no reliable figures for the number of people who are present in the United Kingdom without authorisation (a group which overlaps with but is not the same as unauthorised workers).[4] By subtracting the number of persons known to be in the United Kingdom lawfully from the number of foreign-born people recorded in the 2001 census, the Home Office has come up with a rough estimate that there are between 310,000 and 570,000 people in the United Kingdom without authorisation.[5] These figures are to be treated with caution, however, since they rely on the dubious assumption that persons unlawfully in the United Kingdom are recorded in the census and on speculative figures from passenger surveys as to the rate of emigration by the legally resident population.

2.5 Where do unauthorised workers come from?

Contrary to the popular perception associating unauthorised workers with migration from the developing world, it is likely that a significant proportion of the unauthorised work in the United Kingdom is done by people from industrialised countries who have a limited form of permission to be in the United Kingdom and overstay. This can be inferred from estimates of the likely composition of the group of people present in the United Kingdom without authorisation. The House of

Lords Select Committee on the European Union has pointed out that it is likely that the majority of those who are present without authorisation in the United Kingdom are overstayers rather than people arriving in the country clandestinely.[6] The Select Committee also concluded that it is likely that "the largest number" of them are "from countries such as the United States which provide the largest number of visitors". The Select Committee reached these conclusions relying upon from figures from Australia. In Australia, one of the few countries carrying out comprehensive arrival and departure checks, it was found that overstayers greatly outnumbered the number of unauthorised entrants and that the greatest number of overstayers were British.

Similar conclusions can be drawn from a recent small-scale Home Office study of people who had been living in the United Kingdom without authorisation and were now in immigration detention. The largest single group were found to be those who had entered on a tourist visa and who had then overstayed, although there were – unsurprisingly – no detainees from industrialised countries.[7]

3 Categories of unauthorised work

This section sets out the main categories of unauthorised worker.

3.1 Overstayers

An overstayer is a person who was granted limited leave to enter or remain in the United Kingdom but remained after the time their leave expired, and who does not have a pending application for the leave to be extended. It can be assumed that non-dependent adults who are in the United Kingdom as overstayers for more than a brief period will be engaged in some form of unauthorised work.[8] The largest number of overstayers is likely to be made up of people who come to the United Kingdom as visitors (visitors are normally given six months' leave to enter) and overstay.

3.2 Persons with a limited entitlement to work

Certain categories of immigrant are allowed to work, but subject to restrictions. Overseas students who come to the United Kingdom for a period of over six months may only work for up to 20 hours a week.[9] Similarly, working holidaymakers must only take work 'incidental to a holiday' and in any event for not more than 12 months during their stay in the United Kingdom.[10] Students and working holidaymakers who exceed their allotted hours are engaging in unauthorised working.

Work permit holders[11] cannot change employer without Home Office authorisation; the six month stay of seasonal agricultural workers is limited to a single operator; and workers entering on the sectors based scheme may change employer but not occupation. If these workers switch beyond the permitted range of employment, they will be engaging in unauthorised work.

3.3 Asylum seekers working without permission

An asylum seeker is a person who has claimed international protection on the basis that their removal from the United Kingdom would breach their fundamental human rights under the Geneva Convention relating to the Status of Refugees 1951 ('the Refugee Convention') or under the European Convention on Human Rights ('ECHR'). In 2003, 49,405 people claimed asylum in the United Kingdom (excluding dependants).[12] As is dealt with in detail in section 7, below, most asylum seekers in the United Kingdom do not have permission to work. An 'employment concession' which allowed asylum seekers to work if they waited for more than six months for an initial decision on their case was withdrawn by the Labour government in July 2002. Changes in February 2005 allow certain asylum seekers to work but only if they have had to wait for more than 12 months for an initial decision.

In addition, certain asylum seekers cannot be removed from the United Kingdom after the exhaustion of their appeals because there are practical impediments to their removal. For example, their home country may not be cooperating with the provision of travel documents on which they can be returned, or they may be too ill or too heavily pregnant to travel, or the Home Office may be unable to find a safe route to get them to an area of their country which is deemed safe for them. Though they may in some cases wait several years before return becomes possible, they are at present granted no status in the United Kingdom and do not have permission to work.

The recent small-scale Home Office study of people in immigration detention found that the majority of the asylum seekers questioned had worked, many of them without authorisation.[13]

3.4 Clandestine entry to the United Kingdom other than by asylum seekers

Perhaps self-evidently, there are no reliable estimates of the number of people entering the United Kingdom clandestinely. The number of people detected seeking to evade border controls has risen sharply and was 47,000 in 2000 compared to 3,300 in 1990.[14] It is not clear however to what extent this rise is simply due to increased detection efforts.

The United Kingdom government and press have tended to blur the distinctions between people traffickers, people smugglers or agents and unauthorised work overall. It is vital to note that there is a distinction between people smuggling and people trafficking. The vast majority of people entering the United Kingdom clandestinely will do so with the assistance of an 'agent' or 'people smuggler'. They have not been trafficked.

The new Protocol to the United Nations Convention against Transnational Organized Crime defines trafficking as follows:

"The recruitment, transportation, transfer, harbouring or receipt of persons, by means of the threat or use of force or other forms of coercion, of abduction, of fraud, of deception, of the abuse of power or of a position of vulnerability or of the giving or receiving of payments or benefits to achieve the consent of a person having control over another person, for the purpose of exploitation. Exploitation shall include, at the minimum, the exploitation or the prostitution of others or other forms of sexual exploitation, forced labour or services, slavery or practices similar to slavery, servitude or the removal of organs."

Trafficking may be for domestic labour, for sexual exploitation or for general labour exploitation.

The crucial distinction between people smuggling and people trafficking is that trafficking involves crossing international borders 'for the purpose of exploitation'. The victims of trafficking do not freely consent to travel, and the traffickers who bring them continue to exert close control over them in the destination country. By contrast, migrants who are smuggled may be at the mercy of unscrupulous agents and some, such as refugees, have no choice except to cross borders illegally, but they nonetheless travel voluntarily. The smugglers or agents who bring them may demand debt repayment, but they do not bring migrants to the United Kingdom 'for the purpose of exploitation'.

4 Unauthorised work and labour exploitation

Because unauthorised work is a heterogeneous phenomenon, it would be misleading to depict all unauthorised work as exploitative or abusive. The presence, type and degree of exploitation varies widely according to the industrial sector, the skill level of the work, the resources of the unauthorised worker, and the degree to which the unauthorised worker is dependent on the employer. Structural factors – such as long sub-contracting chains, labour intensive, non-union sectors, casualised working arrangements and indebtedness to employers who are involved in recruiting and importing labour – all play a major role in exploitative employment relationships. The exploitation of migrant workers is not limited to those engaging in unauthorised work: for example, a study on the exploitation of migrant workers published in 2004 by Citizens' Advice Bureaux gave examples of extreme exploitation of EU nationals and of migrants with work permits who were paid wages far below those specified on their wage permits.[15]

Precarious immigration status or the lack of authorisation to work remain serious impediments to the enjoyment of employment rights, however. Unauthorised workers face major obstacles to labour market mobility: lacking choices, unauthorised workers are more likely to remain in abusive working environments.

The recent Home Office study of people in immigration detention found that those individuals working without authorisation were far more likely to be earning wages below the legal minimum than those working with authorisation, though the sample was so small as to make extrapolation difficult.[16] The study reported payment below the minimum wage for over half those for whom information was available, hours of up to 18-20 hours a day and non-payment of wages.

In a small-scale DTI-sponsored study of ethnic minority restaurants and clothing manufacturers it was found that in the restaurant sector, unauthorised workers were paid the same rate (usually below the national minimum wage) as authorised workers.[17] In the clothing industry, however – ironically in light of the common perception that undocumented workers depress wages – employers were found to be 'subsidising' the payment of the national minimum wage to authorised workers by keeping unauthorised workers 'off the books'. Unauthorised workers in the clothing industry were found to be earning 30 per cent less than their authorised counterparts doing the same job in the same workplace. Clothing manufacturers interviewed for the DTI study explained that "if I paid them all the same, I might as well not hire illegals" and "The whole reason for employing illegal workers is to cut costs, so how can you expect me to pay the same as legal workers?"[18] Clothing manufacturers also cited the pliancy and reliability of unauthorised workers as an incentive for hiring them:

"illegals tend to work much harder than the average workers. They do what is asked of them without question, whereas a legal worker would sometimes question before doing certain jobs."[19]

An employer who is aware of his employee's unauthorised position has a stick to wield over the employee's head, to avoid complaints, unionisation, or even demands for payment. In their study of forced labour in the United Kingdom,[20] Anderson and Rogaly give examples of employers calling in immigration officers against unauthorised workers to avoid the payment of wages:

"A Polish hotel worker for example, described seeing a replacement group of workers waiting in an agent's car, while he and his colleagues were being taken away by immigration officials that he believed the employer had called to avoid paying them their wages... An informant described the case of 16 undocumented Chinese workers working in a factory on 16-hour shifts for 20 days. The factory managers then called immigration when they had finished with them and they were deported, thereby avoiding payment of both the workers and the agency."

The Latin American Workers Association and TGWU, interviewed for this project, gave the example of a Colombian employee fired from a small London bakery after getting pregnant. She was told by her employer that if she complained about her firing, he would notify the immigration authorities that she was in the United Kingdom without authorisation. She nonetheless contacted the TGWU, although the bakery subsequently declared bankruptcy and then opened a new outlet.

The Home Office study of immigration detainees notes that:

"The only interviewee who did take legal steps towards extracting payment from his employer... was arrested when he approached the police. He believed that his employer had informed the police that he had overstayed his work visa when she realised he was going to make a formal complaint."

It also noted that "other respondents reported not being paid or being arrested by immigration authorities in raids the day before they were due to receive wages for periods of one week to one month".[21]

Unions and community activists have given examples to this project of the use or threat of immigration paperwork checks and immigration raids against migrant workers during union organising drives.[22] The examples suggest that not only unauthorised, but also authorised migrant workers are affected.

In 2003, UNISON and the East London Community Organisation launched a campaign to raise pay among 160 domestic, portering and catering staff working for a private contractor at a London hospital. In the period leading up to a strike, the contractor threatened both the union and individual workers who were working without authorisation that immigration papers would be checked. In the week before the strike, workers were asked to produce their papers. Between 10 and 15 staff disappeared overnight without trace. Nonetheless, after two rounds of successful strike action, the contractor agreed to union demands.

In January 2005, the TGWU began an organising campaign in a supermarket in South London, which employed 300 primarily West African and Latin American nationals. Union membership rose from 28 to 121. Managers then called for a re-check of immigration papers based on the May 2004 amendment to the paperwork requirements under section 8 of the Asylum and Immigration Act 1996. When some workers were found to be working without authorisation, immigration officers were called in by the management.

One worker was arrested. 60 members of staff, including those working with authorisation, subsequently left their jobs, many without explanation.

In addition to difficulties in organising, those engaged in unauthorised work are at present both legally and practically unable to enforce many labour rights – as is set out in detail in chapter five below. The illegality of the employment contract is a bar to the bringing of claims to an employment tribunal. Lacking protection from immigration enforcement if they blow the whistle on their employers, unauthorised workers hold a rational fear of reporting abuses.

5 Evaluating government policy

5.1 Criteria

The debate on unauthorised working has been characterised not only by a high degree of controversy and politicisation but also by confusion over whether the United Kingdom owes any obligations at all towards unauthorised workers themselves or whether the United Kingdom's sole objectives must be to deter, detect and curb unauthorised working.

The remaining sections of this chapter examine government policy with respect to unauthorised working and make recommendations with respect to it. We begin with a brief analysis of basic criteria which policies on unauthorised working should meet.

As with the rest of this book, we start from the position that immigration control is a given: we do not seek to engage in the wider debate about the ethics of immigration control or the right to freedom of movement.

We suggest that policies on unauthorised working must be designed and implemented so as to meet the following criteria:

- Policies on unauthorised working must safeguard the fundamental human rights of unauthorised workers and their dependants. Fundamental human rights include freedom of association, freedom from forced labour, freedom from arbitrary detention, freedom from inhuman or degrading treatment or punishment, respect for private and family life, access to justice and freedom from discrimination in access to fundamental rights. This criterion is based on the principle, recognised in the UN Declaration of Human Rights and in the European Convention on Human Rights (which is incorporated into United Kingdom law), that states owe a duty to protect fundamental human rights to persons on their territory regardless of citizenship or legal status.
- Policies on unauthorised working must be humane and not deprive

unauthorised workers and their dependants of basic material needs while on United Kingdom territory. 'Basic material needs' are to be understood to include food, shelter, emergency medical care and childhood education. This principle is recognised in Articles 28 and 30 of the UN Migrant Workers Convention. It is also set out in Recommendation R (2000) 3 of the Committee of Ministers of the Council of Europe, on the Right to the Satisfaction of Basic Material Needs of Persons in Situations of Extreme Hardship.[23]

- Policies on unauthorised working must safeguard fundamental employment standards for all workers on United Kingdom territory, regardless of immigration status. Fundamental employment standards include the minimum wage, hours and days off, overtime, health and safety and protection from discrimination. These rights are set out in the 1961 Council of Europe Social Charter (which Britain has ratified). The principle that these rights should apply to unauthorised workers is reflected in Article 25 of the UN Migrant Workers Convention, which Britain has not ratified, but which is the leading statement of international standards on the rights of migrant workers (see further chapter six, below).
- Policies on unauthorised working must be targeted: they must avoid creating or exacerbating discrimination against ethnic minorities in Britain or against authorised migrant workers.
- Policies on unauthorised working must be based on long-term goals, accurate data and carefully-researched impact assessments. Policy should not be formulated in response to newspaper headlines.

5.2 Overview of current policy

The response from successive United Kingdom governments to unauthorised working has certain characteristics. The United Kingdom's focus on deterring, detecting and curbing unauthorised working has not been matched by efforts to reduce the social exclusion of those unauthorised migrant workers already in the United Kingdom. Policy development on unauthorised working has focused on the enforcement of immigration controls, rather than the enforcement of labour standards. The main exception to this pattern is the recent legislation on gangmasters, which is dealt with in chapter five. Enforcement efforts and the debate around unauthorised work have concentrated exclusively on workers from developing countries and in low-skill work.

6 Regularisation

6.1 Current policy

There have been no attempts to undertake a large-scale regularisation of unauthorised workers or of the undocumented foreign

---

population in the United Kingdom since 1977. The United Kingdom's policy has been, with certain exceptions, to regularise on a rolling, individual, case-by-case basis rather than to engage in 'one-shot' collective regularisations.

There are several policies, both within and outside the Immigration Rules, which permit the regularisation of long-resident individuals. If a person has remained in the United Kingdom for 14 continuous years, whether legally or without authorisation, or has remained in the United Kingdom for 10 continuous years of lawful residence, they will normally be entitled to indefinite leave to remain.[24] A person will normally be granted indefinite leave if they have a child who has been living continuously in the United Kingdom for more than seven years. A person will not normally be removed where they have a genuine and subsisting marriage to a person settled in the United Kingdom, the couple were married and living together continuously in the United Kingdom for two years before any enforcement action began, and it would be unreasonable to expect the settled spouse to relocate.

In addition, people who have remained in the United Kingdom without permission for long periods may, in limited situations, be able to rely on Article 8 of the European Convention on Human Rights ('ECHR') which protects the right to respect for private and family life. A person might be able to rely on Article 8 ECHR to challenge removal if they have formed a family in the United Kingdom, have been resident for a long period, and it is unreasonable to expect other family members to follow them to their home country. However, the protection extended by Article 8 ECHR has been restrictively interpreted by the United Kingdom courts as applying only to 'exceptional' cases.

The United Kingdom has also introduced a number of one-off regularisations for specific groups. There have been two significant regularisation exercises for asylum applicants. The 'backlog clearance exercise' in 1998 allowed asylum seekers who had claimed asylum in 1993, and still had no initial decision on their claim, to get indefinite leave to remain, while at the same time granting four years' leave to remain to asylum seekers who had claimed asylum between 1993 and 1995. More recently, the 'one-off families exercise' permitted families with one dependent aged under 18 as of 2 October 2000 or 23 October 2003 to obtain indefinite leave to remain where the principal claimed asylum prior to 2 October 2000.

The regularisation of domestic workers in 1998-1999 is another exception to the lack of collective regularisation programmes in the United Kingdom.[25] Until 1998, domestic workers entering the United Kingdom only had permission to remain while working for a particular employer. Migrant domestic workers' organisations, principally Waling

Waling (now called the United Workers' Association, a 4,000 member organisation affiliated to the TGWU) and Kalaayan, a support organisation for migrant workers, waged a campaign for over 10 years to change the law. In June 1998, domestic workers were brought under the Immigration Rules, with a status separate from their employers'. At the same time, a regularisation programme was announced for domestic workers, which ran from July 1998 to October 1999. The implementation of the regularisation programme was marred by lengthy delays in Home Office decision-making, by the fears of domestic workers about bringing themselves to the authorities' attention, and by conditions for regularisation that applicants had great difficulty in meeting. Those conditions included the requirement that applicants produce their passports – when many had seen their passports confiscated by their employers – and the requirement that applicants produce letters from their current employers as proof of employment – when many employers were reluctant to sign, as they did not want to pay tax or national insurance. By 1999, only 200 people had been regularised.[26] Nonetheless, the change in the law governing the immigration status of domestic workers and the regularisation provides an example of successful campaigning by migrant workers, community organisations and unions for a shift in immigration policy.

Britain's opening of its labour market to accession state nationals after the EU enlargement on 1 May 2004 has also acted as a *de facto* regularisation. By the end of March 2004, 193,000 accession state nationals had signed up under the Worker Registration Scheme.[27] Of these, 33,350 indicated that they had been in the United Kingdom prior to 1 May 2004, at least some of whom will have worked without authorisation. The former Minister for Immigration, Des Browne has praised the benefits of regularisation for accession state nationals:

> "People from the accession states already here have legitimised their position by registering with the scheme and are now contributing to our economy, paying tax and National Insurance but also benefiting from the protections of our employment and health and safety laws."[28]

6.2 Comment and recommendations

The lack of large-scale regularisation programmes in the United Kingdom is in strong contrast to the introduction of collective regularisation programmes in other industrialised countries. Regularisation schemes have been implemented in Belgium (1999), France (1997-1998), Greece (1998 and 2001), Italy (1995-1996, 1998-99 and 2002), Luxembourg (2001), Portugal (1996 and 2001) Spain (1996, 2000, 2001 and 2005) and the United States (1986).[29] Large numbers of persons have also benefited from these schemes. In Greece, it is estimated that 598,000 permits were issued in the 1998 and 2001 exercises.[30] In Italy, there have been 1.4 million successful applications for regularisation in five schemes since 1986, including 634,000 in the 2002 exercise.[31] The 2000 and 2001 schemes in Spain led to 375,000 successful applications, while the most recent scheme, which ran from February to May 2005, led to 700,000 applications.[32]

The cost of the United Kingdom's 'regularisation by stealth' approach is that, while avoiding the controversy associated with large-scale regularisations, most unauthorised workers in the United Kingdom remain in legal limbo. The requirements in the individual routes to regularisation under present law and policy are too restrictive and the qualifying periods too long to assist most unauthorised workers in the short term.

Notwithstanding public indications to this effect, the authorities cannot deal with unauthorised immigrants and unauthorised workers by removals alone. The level of removals remains low. Even if large-scale removals were feasible, it is likely that the effect on community relations would be highly damaging, and that there would be a wrenching effect on families, particularly those with mixed-immigration-status, and long-resident individuals.

As the House of Lords Select Committee on the European Union has said:

> "Some form of regularisation is unavoidable if a growing underclass of people in an unauthorised situation, who are vulnerable to exploitation, is not to be created. It is in the interests of society as a whole that long-term residents should not remain in an unauthorised position."[33]

A large-scale regularisation would have several clear benefits. It would lessen the marginalisation of and extend the coverage of fundamental employment rights and protections to a large swathe of the United Kingdom workforce. There is evidence from the United States that the large-scale regularisation of 1986 improved the wages and labour market opportunities of regularised migrant workers in the United States by increasing their labour market mobility,[34] and that it encouraged greater immigrant integration and the acquisition of education and training by regularised migrant workers. Regularisation can act as a vital source of information on the size, composition and distribution of the unauthorised United Kingdom population. If accompanied by campaigns of education as to employment rights and campaigns of unionisation, it could also facilitate the identification and pursuit of abusive employers. Regularisation would in addition increase revenue from income tax and national insurance.

Regularisation should not, however, be presented as a 'magic bullet' solution to unauthorised immigration or unauthorised working. There is no evidence to show that large-scale regularisations reduce the level of unauthorised working. On the contrary, studies have suggested that the level of unauthorised working rose in the US economy after the 1986 regularisation programme.[36] In European countries which have adopted a large-scale regularisation, despite the regularisation being billed as 'one-off' or 'exceptional', the regularisation has often been repeated a few years later. It has been suggested that a primary reason for the repeat regularisations in Western and Southern Europe has been, in addition to low take-up of early regularisations, that regularisations have often led only to short-term status, with many migrants falling back into unauthorised work when their short-term regular status lapses.[37] Moreover, if the labour market and immigration policy conditions which give rise to unauthorised work are not addressed, there is an obvious possibility that new unauthorised workers will move in to replace the old.

We recommend a collective regularisation as the only means to prevent the long-term marginalisation and exclusion of the United Kingdom's unauthorised worker population.

We propose that regularisation should be based on proof of presence rather than on proof of employment, to avoid handing a veto to employers over whether their employees are able to access regular status. There should be a requirement of two years' presence in the United Kingdom: sufficiently long to focus regularisation on those who have put down roots in the United Kingdom, but sufficiently short to ensure maximum coverage. We also recommend that regularisation should include those who have temporary admission as asylum seekers, and who remain in the asylum appeals system, or who have exhausted their appeals, provided they meet the qualifying time period. Asylum seekers should not however have to renounce any extant rights of appeal.

We recommend that regularisation offer migrant workers a route to permanent status, both as an incentive to integration and the acquisition of human capital, and in order to prevent workers relapsing into unauthorised status on the expiry of a short-term permit. However, we do not propose that applicants should immediately obtain permanent residence. Not all regularising migrants will seek permanent status; and the immediate grant of permanent status would be incompatible with the current United Kingdom framework of short term work permits and short term grants of humanitarian protection and discretionary leave.

We therefore recommend a tiered process of 'earned regularisation' which blends elements of the US and French experience (where regularisation has led immediately to permanent residence) and the Southern European experience (where regularisations have led to short term permits).[38] Applicants would first obtain temporary residence and work permission under broad criteria, on registering and establishing that they have lived in the country for the qualifying period. On completion of the temporary residence period, applicants would, on showing stable formal sector employment, be eligible for permanent residence. We recommend that the period before eligibility for permanent residence should be the same as for work permit holders (currently four years). A further filter which could be built into such a programme would be to require temporary permit holders to apply for a renewal of the temporary permit half way to becoming eligible to seek indefinite leave to remain, and to show stable formal sector employment at that point.

7 Asylum seekers' access to the labour market

7.1 Current policy

Between 1986 and 2002, asylum seekers were given permission to work if they had to wait more than six months for their applications to be decided by the Home Secretary. That 'employment concession' for asylum seekers was ended by the Labour government in July 2002 in response to public fears about abuse of the asylum system by economic migrants. As Lord Filkin, then a Home Office Minister, told the House of Lords in a convoluted statement:

"There is a perceived belief that those who do not have a well-founded fear of persecution but wish to come here for economic reasons are claiming asylum because they believe that this will allow them to work here. While that was not the case, we must take steps to ensure that people do not make fraudulent applications for asylum."[39]

Aside from those asylum seekers who had been granted and retained permission to work under the old 'concession', and aside from exceptional cases, asylum seekers no longer had permission to work.

The United Kingdom's position on labour market access for asylum seekers changed again in February 2005 in order to comply with Council Directive 2003/9 of 27 January 2003 on minimum standards for the reception of asylum seekers. Article 11 of the Directive requires member states to "decide the conditions for granting access to the labour market" to asylum seekers if they have to wait for more than 12 months for a decision at first instance. The government exercised its right to opt into the Directive, and during the negotiations was a strong advocate of the principle in Article 11. Article 11 has been implemented by the new paragraph 360 of the Immigration Rules, which allows asylum seekers to apply for permission to take employment if they have been waiting for more than 12 months for an initial decision on their asylum claim and the delay 'cannot be attributed to the applicant himself'. This does not, however, extend to include permission to be self-employed or to engage in business activity.

There is a separate issue concerning asylum seekers who (as was set out in section 3.3) having exhausted their appeals, cannot be returned to their state of nationality due to practical impediments such as illness, lack of cooperation from their home government or the lack of a safe return route. State support through the National Asylum Support Service ('NASS') is usually withdrawn from these asylum seekers 21 days after the final decision on their asylum or human rights appeal. Those who cannot be returned to their home country are eligible for 'hard cases support', which is limited to the provision of food and accommodation. They are not allowed to work. Section 10 of the Asylum and Immigration (Treatment of Claimants, etc) Act 2004 now empowers the Home Office to require them to do community work as a condition of receiving accommodation.

7.2 Comment and recommendations

The February 2005 change in the Immigration Rules will affect only a small number of asylum seekers. This is because the change only provides permission to work for those who suffer long delays in waiting for an initial Home Office decision. The wait for an initial decision has fallen, with the most recent official statistics showing that 77 per cent of applications made in the final quarter of 2004 had the initial Home Office decision reached and served within two months.[40] Though the Asylum and Immigration Treatment of Claimants etc Act 2004 has sharply speeded up the appeals process, asylum seekers may still remain in the appeals process for extended periods. Where delays do take place, it is usually during the appeals process.

The position remains therefore, that most asylum seekers do not have permission to work. In most cases, asylum seekers' only lawful recourse is to support from the National Asylum Support Service ('NASS') or to support from members of their families and communities. As of March 2005, a single person of 25 or over was entitled to £38.96 a week in NASS support. This amounts to 70 per cent of the amount available to British citizens. Asylum seekers can be refused

NASS support if they refuse to accept dispersal accommodation: since 2000, asylum seekers are dispersed to allocated accommodation, often at several hours' notice, across the country and away from their legal advisors, their doctors, and their adult children or siblings.

It has been a predictable result of these policies that considerable numbers of asylum seekers are falling back on unauthorised work. The denial of work opportunities to asylum seekers also reinforces public perceptions of asylum seekers as parasitic and living off benefits.

We recommend that all asylum seekers who are still waiting for an initial decision or who are still in the asylum appeals system six months after the date of their initial asylum application should be granted permission to work. Lest it be objected that allowing asylum seekers to work if the appeals process becomes protracted provides an incentive for asylum seekers to bring spurious appeals, we would point out that there are increasingly stringent thresholds to be crossed before an asylum seeker can appeal. We also recommend that there should be discretion to grant permission to work to asylum seekers within a shorter time scale. We recommend that permission to work should extend to self-employment and business activities.

Reform is also required as to the treatment of asylum seekers who have failed in their appeals but who cannot be returned, and who do not have permission to work. There are acute difficulties with 'hard cases support'. Its availability is not widely publicised, it is difficult to access, and there are frequent delays between the termination of NASS provision and the commencement of hard cases support. As a result, asylum seekers who cannot be removed frequently become destitute.

The new compulsory community service measure for 'hard cases' in section 10 of the Asylum and Immigration (Treatment of Claimants etc) Act 2004 also risks making destitute those non-returnable asylum seekers who refuse to or cannot work. It is likely to reinforce public associations of asylum seekers with criminality: the only modern-day parallel for compulsory community work is in the criminal justice system. It also risks reinforcing public notions that asylum seekers – who are in fact denied permission to work – are parasitic and have to be forced to work. As the Parliamentary Joint Committee for Human Rights has pointed out, there is also a "significant risk" that section 10 breaches the prohibitions on forced labour and on inhuman and degrading treatment in the European Convention of Human Rights.[41]

We recommend that these asylum seekers who have exhausted their appeals but who are non-returnable be granted temporary status which provides permission to work. As the Home Affairs Select Committee has stated in making the same proposal:

"We believe it is absurd to refuse leave to remain to people who, for whatever reason, cannot be removed. We recommend that such people be granted a temporary status which will allow them to support themselves."[42]

We also recommend the repeal of section 10 of the 2004 Act.

8 Immigration control in the workplace

8.1 Current policy

Until 1997, there were no penalties for the employers of unauthorised workers. The Conservative government argued on introducing them that criminal penalties for employers would act as a deterrent to unauthorised immigration.[43] It is now a criminal offence under section 8 of the Asylum and Immigration Act 1996 to employ a person who does not have a right to work in the United Kingdom or who does not have a right to do the particular form of work. The offence is punishable by fines of up to £5,000 per employee – although, in practice the fine is usually substantially lower.

There is a statutory defence for an employer charged with a section 8 offence, that, before the employment began, the employer saw and retained or copied specified documents. The defence does not apply where the employer knew that the employee was not, in fact, entitled to work. The list of documents was modified, rendering the requirements more stringent, with effect from 1 May 2004.[44]

Employers are very rarely prosecuted for this offence and still more rarely convicted. In the 1998-2003 period there were only 24 prosecutions in England and Wales, leading to only nine convictions.[45] Employers can escape prosecution by co-operating with the authorities.

In February 2005 the government proposed significant changes to the system of penalties for the employers of unauthorised workers: these are now included in the Immigration Asylum and Nationality Bill 2005. If passed, the provisions in the Asylum and Nationality Bill 2005 would replace section 8 of the 1996 Act with two separate measures. There would be an 'on-the-spot' civil penalty, payable within 14 days for the employers of unauthorised workers who are unable to show that they complied with 'prescribed requirements' of examining and retaining copies of documents.[46] The Bill does not specify what the civil penalty would be but the government has suggested a fine of £2,000 per unauthorised employee. As a civil rather than criminal penalty, the burden would be on the employer to establish his 'innocence' in the County Court if he wanted to challenge the fine. There would also be a separate criminal offence of knowingly employing a person without authorisation.[47] The penalties under the proposed new criminal offence are considerably harsher than those under section 8 of the 1996 Act. If introduced, the criminal offence would be punishable on summary conviction by a fine of up to £5,000 and/or imprisonment for up to one year; and, on indictment, by a fine and/or imprisonment for up to two years. The details of the checks which employers must make, and of the factors to be taken into account in deciding on the amount of the fine, remain to be announced at the time of writing.

A separate government proposal – the introduction of national identity cards – also has wide-reaching implications for workplace immigration controls.[48] The government's current plan is to introduce identity cards and registration on the related National Identity Register in two phases – first by tying it to the issuing of other documents, and then by making it compulsory for all residents. In the first phase, most non-British residents will have to register and obtain an identity document based on biometric technology. It is only in the second phase that that obligation will be generalised to British nationals. If and when they come into operation, identity cards and the National Identity Register are to have many functions, including becoming a requirement for access to public services. The government's intention is that identity cards and the register will be used to "tackle" unauthorised work. It is highly likely that, if introduced, the identity card and register system will be linked to employer penalties.

It is to be anticipated that any introduction of 'on the spot' fines – or eventually of identity cards – would be accompanied by the enhanced use of immigration raids on workplaces. There has already been a sharp rise in the resources devoted to enforcement actions against unauthorised work. Between 2002 and 2004, the number of staff involved in enforcement actions rose by 50 per cent.[49] In 2004, the Home Office reported that

> "Between April and June 2003 the Immigration Service reported carrying out 79 illegal working operations of which 27 were aimed at detecting five or more illegal workers. Between October and November last year the number of reported operations increased by over 75 per cent on the second quarter to 141, while the operations aimed at detecting five or more illegal workers rose by over 175 per cent to 75."[50]

8.2 Comment and recommendations

Penalties on employers who hire unauthorised workers are significant in that they turn employers into frontline enforcers of immigration control, by effectively requiring that they check the immigration status of employees who appear to be immigrants.

At the time section 8 of the Asylum and Immigration Act 1996 was introduced, both the TUC and the Commission for Racial

Equality criticised it as likely to increase discrimination against minority job applicants. Evidence of the accuracy of this prediction can be found in the recent Employment Appeal Tribunal case of *Olatokun v Ikon Office Solutions.*[51] The employer there had a policy of asking all job applicants for their place of birth and of then asking those born outside the EU to provide documents showing they were entitled to work. The applicant was a Nigerian woman who had indefinite leave to remain and therefore did not require permission to work. She had been working as office-coordinator for four months when her employers sent her a form asking for her place of birth. On finding that she was born in Nigeria, they asked to see her passport. However the applicant was in the process of applying for British citizenship and had sent her passport to the Home Office. Though she provided a letter from the Home Office showing that she had indefinite leave to remain in the United Kingdom, she was dismissed. The EAT found that the employer had not discriminated by asking only job applicants born outside the EU to show their papers. That was because this was an act which the employer had undertaken in order to comply with obligations under section 8 of the Asylum and Immigration Act 1996, and was therefore protected by section 41 of the Race Relations Act.

Very similar legislation in the US ('employer sanctions' under the 1986 US Immigration Reform and Control Act) was found to have resulted in a sharp rise in discriminatory practices against workers of foreign appearance. The US General Accounting Office carried out a large-sample survey in 1990 which found that the introduction of criminal sanctions against the employers of unauthorised workers had resulted in "widespread discrimination" and "a serious pattern of discrimination".[52] It estimated that, as a result of the legislation, 10 per cent of US employers had adopted discriminatory practices, including refusing to hire workers who seemed to the employer to be foreign, and that these practices affected not only unauthorised workers, but those eligible to work.

As was seen above in section 4 of this chapter, employer penalties may also affect the ability of both authorised and unauthorised workers to make complaints or unionise. There are no prohibitions on employers demanding to see immigration-related paperwork from a foreign-born employee who has, for example, sought to unionise his or her workplace or on raids during union organising drives. There are also no protections for whistleblowers: unauthorised workers who complain to government bodies over breaches of health and safety provisions or failure to pay the minimum wage have no protection from immigration enforcement.

In the US, the increasing penetration of immigration control to the workplace has been found to seriously detract from the ability of migrant workers to organise. In its study of freedom of association in the United States, Human Rights Watch reported that they had

"found repeated use of threats by employers during National Labour Relations Board campaigns to call the Immigration and Naturalisation Service to have workers deported if they formed and joined a union... The precarious situation of undocumented immigrants inhibits workers' freedom of association on a national scale."[53]

A Director of Recruitment for the AFL-CIO Organising Institute (the organiser training academy of the US trade union federation) has described how:

"Right in the middle of an organising drive, employers will announce 'everybody bring in their papers tomorrow, we're having a paper check'. Often the employer doesn't even have to fire the workers. When the employer announces a paper check, a lot of workers just quit on the spot, for fear that the employer will call the Immigration Service and they will be deported. And when a group of workers is fired, or quits during the organising process, people feel powerless, that there is no way they can fight for change."[54]

The AFL-CIO, which had campaigned for decades for the introduction of criminal sanctions against the employers of unauthorised workers reversed its policy in February 2000 and is calling for the repeal of the legislation. In 2001, AFL-CIO President John Sweeney testified to the United States Senate that:

"Even though the object of employer sanctions was to punish employers who knowingly hire undocumented workers, and not the workers themselves, in reality employers have manipulated the program to violate federal and state labor laws and to discriminate against workers. The current situation not only harms all workers, but also those employers who face unfair competition from others who skimp on labor costs by hiring and then exploiting undocumented workers... Although employer sanctions did not create the problems of exploitation and discrimination, they have contributed significantly to the inability of immigrant workers to enjoy and enforce the most basic of labor and workplace rights. Having failed to fulfill their central purposes and, indeed, having set back the progress of workers generally, employer sanctions must be repealed."[55]

There is no evidence either that the imposition of criminal penalties for employing unauthorised workers is an effective deterrent to unauthorised working. A 20-country survey of employer sanctions by the US General Accounting Office in 1982 concluded that even where high penalties, including jail, are imposed on employers, sanctions are not effective deterrents to hiring unauthorised workers.[56] In the US, where the measure has been in place for a decade longer than in the United Kingdom, employer sanctions have failed to make any dent in the population of unauthorised workers. 2003 estimates from the US Census Bureau placed the undocumented population of the United States at between nine and 10 million, and growing at between 300,000 and 500,000 per year.

The encroachment of immigration control on the workplace weakens the ability of migrant workers to enjoy fundamental employment rights, causes maximum disruption and fear and is not targeted but potentially affects all migrant workers regardless of whether they have regular or irregular status. These problems will not be resolved and are likely to be significantly exacerbated by adding more immigration raids, by imposing heavier criminal penalties or by introducing a new 'on the spot' civil penalty.

As is already the position of the TUC, we recommend that criminal penalties against the employers of unauthorised workers should be abolished rather than added to. We also strongly oppose the introduction of the intended 'on the spot' civil penalty for the employers of unauthorised workers.

This is not the place for a comprehensive examination of the identity cards proposal with its wide-reaching ramifications for relations between the individual and state in the United Kingdom. We nevertheless record our serious concerns at the potential exchange of information between agencies without the knowledge or consent of the individual, the risks that identity cards will have a discriminatory impact, and the danger that identity cards will create an underclass of unauthorised persons, denied access to non-emergency public services. In the employment context, we have doubts that this measure will reduce unauthorised working. Employers who do not currently check immigration papers are unlikely to do so upon the introduction of a compulsory identity card. At the same time, the introduction of an identity card risks driving those present or working without authorisation further underground. We therefore strongly oppose the introduction of compulsory identity cards.

9 Trafficking for exploitation

9.1 Current policy

Section 145 of the Nationality, Immigration and Asylum Act 2002 created a new offence of trafficking in prostitution, punishable by up to 14 years' imprisonment on indictment. That offence is now set

---

out in sections 57, 58 and 59 of the Sexual Offences Act 2003. In addition, section 4 of the Asylum and Immigration (Treatment of Claimants, etc) Act 2004 created a new offence of trafficking people for exploitation, including for the purposes of forced labour, again punishable by up to 14 years' imprisonment.

Home Office circular 12/97 allows the Home Office to temporarily regularise the immigration status of victims of trafficking. As is discussed below, in practice this protection is only available for persons who are admitted to the Poppy Scheme – a shelter for women only.

European-wide measures to protect the victims of people trafficking have not been adopted by the United Kingdom. The United Kingdom opted out of the Council Directive 2004/81. It requires Member States (other than the United Kingdom, Ireland and Denmark) to provide victims of trafficking and persons who have been smuggled, who cooperate with the authorities, with short term residential permits of at least six months' duration. The Directive on victims of trafficking not only provides for a temporary residential status for the victims of people trafficking, but also provides a temporary residential status for those who cooperate in the prosecution of people smugglers.

9.2 Comment and recommendations

In the area of people trafficking, the government's emphasis has been on the interception and prosecution of people traffickers rather than the protection and rehabilitation of victims of trafficking, including people who have been trafficked into forced labour.

The sole existing shelter for victims of trafficking, the Poppy Scheme, has 25 beds. The restrictive Poppy Scheme criteria are targeted at obtaining cooperation in catching traffickers in sex workers. The Poppy Scheme is only for those who have been trafficked into prostitution, who were in prostitution within the last 30 days, who were brought directly to the United Kingdom and who express willingness to cooperate with the United Kingdom authorities. Those victims of trafficking who are picked up and who do not meet the Poppy Scheme criteria (or who apply when the Project is full) are liable to be detained at Oakington detention centre and to have any claims against removal dealt with under the fast track scheme.

Though it provides a helpful starting point, the Council Directive on the victims of trafficking provides only heavily qualified rights for the victims of trafficking and smuggling. For example, the Directive makes the residence permit conditional on the third country national's continued usefulness in a criminal investigation or prosecution: the residence permit can be withdrawn if the third country national ceases to cooperate with criminal investigations or if the proceedings are discontinued.

We recommend that the United Kingdom adopt and implement Council Directive 2004/81 on the residence permit issued to third country nationals who are the victims of trafficking in human beings. We also recommend going beyond the rights provided by the Directive for the victims of trafficking. We recommend that after a reflection period, victims of trafficking who agree to cooperate in the provision of information should be granted a six month residence permit which would only be terminated within the six months in exceptional circumstances (fraud or national security reasons).

We also recommend the expansion of the present shelter scheme to new shelters, to include victims of people trafficking other than for sexual exploitation, and to include those trafficked via other countries to the United Kingdom.

10 Conclusion

Other recommendations of relevance to unauthorised working are dealt with elsewhere in this book. Chapter three proposes the expansion of regular channels of migration, chapter four proposes that unauthorised workers should be able to enforce employment standards, while chapter six proposes the ratification of the UN Migrant Workers Convention.

This chapter has suggested that in order to reduce the exploitative treatment of both unauthorised and authorised migrant workers, new emphasis must be placed on labour standards enforcement. This means that employers must not be required or permitted to become the enforcers of immigration controls, and that unauthorised workers who unionise, bring complaints against their employers or seek to enforce labour standards in their workplaces must be protected from the retaliatory use of immigration enforcement.

The point has also been made here that the government must be tough not on unauthorised workers but on the causes of unauthorised work within the United Kingdom. The government must deal with employer demand by taking steps to reduce the vulnerability to exploitation and exclusion from fundamental employment protections which create perverse incentives for employers to hire unauthorised workers. Addressing the causes of unauthorised work also means permitting the regularisation of unauthorised workers who have been in the United Kingdom for long periods and lifting the bars to work by certain groups of migrants.

Notes

1   D Davis, 'Labour's refusal to tackle illegal immigration is hurting everyone', *Mail on Sunday,* 15 February 2005.
2   Economic and Social Committee Opinion on the European Commission's communication on a Common Policy on Immigration, CES 527/2002, para 2.1.
3   Conversely, not all migrant workers in the informal economy are working without authorisation.
4   For an evaluation of alternative methodologies for measuring this population, see: G Mclaughlan, C Pinkerton and J Salt, *Sizing the Illegally Resident Population in the United Kingdom* (Home Office, 2004).
5   J Woodbridge, *Sizing the Unauthorised (Illegal) Migrant Population in the United Kingdom in 2001,* Home Office Online Report 29/05.
6   House of Lords Select Committee on the European Union, *A Common Policy on Illegal Immigration* 37th Report, 2001-2002, para 20.
7   R Black, M Collyer, R Skelton, C Waddington *A survey of the illegally resident population in detention in the United Kingdom* Home Office Online Report 20/05 ('Black et al').
8   Black et al found that 75 per cent of the respondents, all of whom were present in the United Kingdom without authorisation, had worked at some point: see their Ch 5. This figure does however include those who were working with authorisation and then subsequently overstayed.
9   In 2003, 319,000 students entered the United Kingdom: Home Office, 'Control of Immigration: Statistics – United Kingdom 2003', Home Office Statistical Bulletin 12/04, Table 1.2.
10 In 2003, 46,500 working holiday makers entered the United Kingdom: Ibid.
11 In 2003, 119,000 work permit holders entered the United Kingdom: Ibid.
12 Ibid, Table 2.2.
13 Black et al, Ch 5.
14 Home Office, *Secure Borders, Safe Haven: integration with diversity in modern Britain* (2002), p. 76.
15 Citizens' Advice Bureaux, *Nowhere to Turn – CAB Evidence on the Exploitation of Migrant Workers* (London, 2004).
16 Black et al, Ch 5.
17 M Ram, P Edwards and T Jones, *Employers and Illegal Migrant Workers in the Clothing and Restaurant Sectors* (London: Department of Trade and Industry, 2002).
18 Ibid, p 26.
19 Ibid, p 27.
20 B Anderson and B Rogaly, *Forced Labour and Migration to the UK,* (London: TUC, 2005) p 47.
21 Black et al, p 28.
22 Our thanks to the TGWU, the Latin American Workers Association and UNISON for their help with the empirical material relied upon in this section.
23 For a detailed analysis, see R Cholewinski 'Study on Obstacles to Effective Access of Irregular Migrants to Minimum Social Rights', Council of Europe document CDMG (2004) 29 (November 2004).
24 Paragraph 276A of the Immigration Rules.
25 See B Anderson, *Doing the Dirty Work: the global politics of domestic labour* (London: Zed Books, 2000), Ch 6.
26 A Levinson 2005, *The Regularisation of Unauthorised Migrants, Literature Survey and Country Case Studies* (Oxford: COMPAS, 2005), p 30.
27 Home Office and other departments, *Accession Monitoring Report May 2004-March 2005* (May 2005).

28 'Worker Registration Scheme and Work Permit Figures Published', WPUK press release, 24 February 2005

29 See Levinson, Part II.

30 Ibid, Table 6, p 35.

31 Ibid, Table 8, p 40.

32 Ibid, p 49 and 'Spain grants amnesty to 700,000 migrants', *The Guardian*, 9 May 2005.

33 House of Lords Select Committee on the European Union, *A Common Policy on Illegal Immigration* 37th Report, 2001-2002, para 112.

34 D Cobb-Clark and S Kossoudiji, 'IRCA's impact on the occupational concentration and mobility of newly-legalised Mexican Men' (2000) 13 *Journal of Population Economics*; and D Cobb-Clark and S Kossoudiji, 'Coming out of the Shadows: Learning about Legal Status and Wages from the Legalised Population' (2002) 20 *Journal of Labour Economics* 598.

35 P Orrenius and M Zavodny 'Do Amnesty Programmes Encourage Illegal Immigration? Evidence from IRCA' *Federal Reserve Bank of Dallas Working Paper* 103, 2001.

36 Levinson, p 18.

37 Ibid, p 9.

38 These proposals are adapted from recommendations in Migration Policy Institute *Managing Irregular Migration*, Policy Brief 4 (Washington DC: 2004).

39 House of Lords, 24 October 2002.

40 Home Office, *Asylum Statistics:* 1st Quarter 2005, p 4.

41 Joint Committee on Human Rights of the House of Lords/House of Commons, *Fourteenth Report*, 2003-04, paras 9-16.

42 House of Commons Home Affairs Select Committee, Fourth Report, Asylum Removals, 14 April 2003

43 For a detailed account of the introduction of section 8, see B Ryan 'Employer Enforcement of Immigration Law after Section Eight of the Asylum and Immigration Act 1996' (1997) 26 *Industrial Law Journal* 136.

44 Immigration (Restrictions on Employment) Order, SI 2004/755.

45 Home Office, *Control of Immigration Statistics 2002,* Table 7.5 and *Control of Immigration Statistics 2003,* Table 6.5.

46 Clause 11 of the Immigration, Asylum and Nationality Bill, as introduced on 22 June 2005.

47 Clause 17 of the Immigration, Asylum and Nationality Bill, as introduced on 22 June 2005.

48 Home Office, *Legislation in Identity Cards: A Consultation* (Cm 6178, April 2004).

49 'New measures to tackle illegal working' Immigration and Nationality Directorate press release, 16 March 2004.

50 Home Office Minister, Baroness Scotland, House of Lords, 11 February 2004.

51 UKEAT/0074/04, 10 May 2004.

52 General Accounting Office, *Immigration Reform: Employer Sanctions and the Question of Discrimination* (Washington DC, 1990).

53 Human Rights Watch, *Unfair Advantage, Workers Freedom of Association in the United States* (New York, 2000).

54 Interview conducted in 2000, cited in L Dubinsky and S Luebke, 'USA Unions and Immigration', (2000) 7 *International Union Rights* 20-21.

55 Testimony of John Sweeney to the US Senate Committee on the Judiciary, 7 September 2001.

56 General Accounting Office, *Information on the Enforcement of Laws Regarding Employment of Aliens in Selected Countries* (Washington DC, 1982).

Chapter 4 : **Unauthorised working**

Chapter 5

Migrant workers and employment law

1 Introduction

As was explained in chapter one, an analysis of policy with respect to migrant workers requires a consideration not just of immigration rules, but also of employment law. Are migrant workers covered by the same rights and standards as other workers? Are they able to enforce the rights and standards which do apply to them? Are there changes to employment law which are made necessary by the situation of migrant workers? These are the questions which this chapter sets out to address.

At the outset, it is important to recognise the significance for *all* workers of the question of the adequacy of the employment law framework relating to migrants. An acceptable level of protection is firstly a matter of great of importance to migrant workers themselves. They have the same interest as other workers in decent conditions at work, a safe working environment and in ensuring that employers honour their legal and contractual commitments. At the same time, the protection of migrant workers is of interest to others. Where the weakness of employment law permits employers to engage in the abusive exploitation of migrant workers, this undermines the position of all workers. Securing the effectiveness of employment law for migrant workers is both an act of solidarity with them and an attempt to ensure a level playing field within the labour market.

The first part of the chapter offers a discussion of three general issues to do with the framework of labour law, and which are of particular relevance to migrant workers. We argue for the rejection of the doctrine of illegality, which prevents the enforcement of the contract itself and of statutory employment rights, in relation to workers whose employment is inconsistent with immigration law. We highlight the need for greater control of intermediaries in the labour market – ie. agencies and gangmasters – if migrant workers are to be effectively protected. We also propose that the coverage of all employment rights be extended to all workers, as that too is likely to be of particular concern to migrant workers. In the second part of the chapter, we then provide a detailed analysis of the key employment rights, and show how the situation of migrant workers requires these rights to be strengthened.

The premise on which this chapter is based is that there are some employment rights which are so essential to worker protection that they should apply in all circumstances, regardless of the worker's immigration status. The chapter identifies problems with the content of the law which the presence of migrant workers throws into question – above all, in the limits to the legal protection available to casual and lower paid workers. In this, the report bears out the analysis of the Institute of Employment Rights in its many other publications which have documented the deficiencies in current United Kingdom employment law. Nothing that is highlighted in this chapter is however intended to imply that United Kingdom employment legislation is otherwise adequate, or that the only area of contention is over how it impacts on the rights of migrant workers.

2 The framework of labour law

2.1 Unauthorised workers and labour law

United Kingdom law takes a tough line on the capacity of workers who work in breach of immigration requirements to enforce employment laws. This is because the legal approach to the question starts from the common law doctrine of illegality, that a person should not be able to profit from their wrong. In practice, the doctrine operates both in relation to those working without paying tax or national insurance contributions, and in relation to those employed without permission under immigration law. The consequence is to allow employers to avoid their duties and liabilities to those they employ, making it advantageous to them to encourage illegal contracts.

The British courts have long held that workers who are covered by the doctrine of illegality cannot enforce either the employment contract or statutory rights, such as protection against unfair dismissal, which depend upon it. It had previously been thought that workers covered by the doctrine of illegality could nevertheless rely upon statutory protection against discrimination, as that was said to

> ## Unenforceable rights
>
> X, who comes from China, had got into difficulties with debt, when his business was ruined after an accident. Debt collectors were threatening him. X entered the United Kingdom without permission having paid a large amount of money to traffickers to get a passport. He says that it will take him five to six years just to pay off this debt. His aim is to try and make as much money as possible to pay off his debts and to provide for his family back home. He has two children, a 14 year old and 12 year old.
>
> He starts at 11am, works until 2pm has a two hour break and then works from 4pm to 11.30pm six days a week. X earns £240 a week (around £4 an hour – well below the national minimum wage) and sends most of it home except for a small amount for his own daily expenditure.
>
> *Source: Working Lives Research Institute, East of England project 2005*

be independent of the contract of employment. That view was supported in particular by the decision of the Employment Appeal Tribunal in *Leighton v Michael* in 1995.[1]

In July 2004, however, in *Vakante v Addey and Stanhope School*,[2] the Court of Appeal rejected the claim that a Croatian national who worked in breach of immigration laws could bring proceedings under the Race Relations Act. It endorsed the approach to the operation of the doctrine of illegality set out previously in the case of *Hall v Woolston Hall Leisure*,[3] which concerned non-payment by an employer of taxes and national insurance contributions. That approach is as follows:

"to consider whether the applicant's claim arises out of or is so clearly connected or inextricably bound up or linked with the illegal conduct of the applicant that the court could not permit the applicant to recover compensation without appearing to condone that conduct."

Faced with a worker taking employment in breach of immigration law, that principle could only lead to one result. While the court accepted that public policy favoured protection against discrimination for workers, even if there were elements of illegality in their contracts, in this case the court highlighted that the illegal conduct was criminal, that it went to the heart of the employment situation, and that the consequences of that illegality lay solely at the door of the applicant. Its conclusion was that in cases where the illegality is entirely down to the worker – as seems likely in cases of a breach of immigration law – there was no right to claim protection against discrimination.

Vakante is a worrying decision for those who support the enforcement of employment laws. What it means is that unauthorised workers are now unable to enforce *any* employment rights which depend upon their making an individual legal claim. Among other things, they cannot enforce their contracts of employment, secure payment of minimum wages, allege discrimination by employers, claim unfair dismissal, or assert that an employer has breached their trade union rights. In employment law terms, they are treated as non-persons.

Our recommendation is that unauthorised workers should not be deprived of employment rights. In the first place, such a state of affairs has serious practical consequences for workers. It gives a green light to employers to employ workers without permission to work, secure in the knowledge that they cannot complain about subsequent mistreatment, or failure to respect the terms of the agreement. Legal claims are ruled out, workers can be dismissed with impunity if they complain about their treatment, and there is no protection for collective action which workers might engage in. We also recommend, that for the avoidance of doubt, the *Hall* and *Vakante* rulings should be reversed, so as to make clear that unauthorised workers can enforce anti-discrimination laws.

There are anyway reasons to doubt whether the rigid application of the doctrine of illegality in this context is consistent with a policy of discouraging unauthorised immigration. The truth may well be the reverse. By denying the basic protections of employment law to unauthorised workers, the legal position creates an incentive for employers to hire them. When it comes to employment rights, ignoring illegality of conduct may actually be the best way to reduce it.

There is also growing support in international law for the principle that unauthorised workers should be covered by employment law and social security. It has for example been held contrary to International Labour Organisation principles on freedom of association to exclude unauthorised workers from trade union rights.[4] Reference may be made here in particular to Article 25 of the UN Convention on the Protection of the Rights of Migrant Workers and their Families. Article 25 begins by providing for the right of migrant workers to equal treatment in all aspects of employment conditions. It then goes on to state that "employers shall not be relieved of any legal or contractual obligations" as a result of the irregularity of the status of workers. Although Britain has not ratified this Convention, it is the fullest expression of international consensus as to the protections to which migrant workers should be entitled (see further chapter six, below).

One further issue which arises concerns the evasion of income tax and national insurance contributions. While we do not wish to condone such practices by workers, or by employers who profit from them, if the employment rights of unauthorised workers are to be safeguarded, it is necessary to protect them from the doctrine of illegality in so far as it concerns the non-payment of taxes and contributions. The position of a worker who has a right to work in Britain, and who chooses to partici-

> ## Agency work
>
> Z couldn't find any work in Poland. He left school at the age of 18 and had wanted to go to university to study economics but didn't have the necessary funds. He came to the United Kingdom looking for any kind of work and has worked on the land, in construction and in factory work.
>
> He is currently working in a potato factory. He works a 60-hour week and got the job through an agency. He earns as little as £4 an hour. Z works long hours – 10-12 on a night shift – and everything that he earns is spent on food and accommodation. He is continually moved from factory to factory because he is working through the agency and only gets work on a daily basis. He and other Polish colleagues paid £300 to what he describes as the "Polish mafia" for access to work.
>
> *Source:Working Lives Research Institute, East of England project 2005*

pate in evasion, is very different to that of an unauthorised worker for whom payment of taxes and contribution may not be a realistic option. We recommend that unauthorised workers be immune from the doctrine of illegality as regards the non-payment of taxes and contributions.

2.2 Gangmasters and agencies

It has become apparent in recent years that gangmasters provide work for many migrant workers, both legal and irregular. A 'gangmaster' is someone who supplies temporary labour for an employer when and where it is needed. While the scale of operations by gangmasters is unknown,[5] what is known is that they frequently exercise a great deal of control over the labour of their workers. They often set the rate of pay that the worker will get, transport workers to the workplace, supervise them while at work, and make arrangements for their accommodation.

In legal terms it can be difficult to separate gangmasters from employment agencies. They perform a similar function, in that both act as intermediaries between workers and employers. In practice too, many migrant workers obtain work through agencies as well as through gangmasters. Accordingly, the discussion here deals with both categories of intermediary together.

a) Regulation

The system of regulation of intermediaries, be they agencies or gangmasters, is the first issue which needs to be addressed. What are the rules governing these activities? Should changes be made, taking into account the position of migrant workers in particular?

The operation of employment agencies is governed by the Employment Agencies Act 1973 and the Conduct of Employment Agencies and Employment Businesses Regulations 2003.[6] This legislation applies both to 'employment agencies', which are in "the business... of finding persons employment with employers or of supplying employers with persons for employment by them", and to 'employment businesses', which employ workers and supply them to third parties.[7] Until January 1995, it was necessary for employment agencies to obtain a licence from the Secretary of State. In order to obtain a licence the applicant had to show that the business premises were suitable, that the business was being properly conducted, and that the individuals running the agency had not been found guilty of any misconduct. The requirement to obtain a licence was however abolished as part of Conservative 'deregulation' efforts. Since 1995, anyone may set up and operate an employment agency without obtaining permission. It is only if a breach of the rules is identified that regulation comes into play – through the imposition of fines, and the possibility for the Secretary of State for Trade and Industry to apply to an employment tribunal for an order barring named individuals from operating an agency.

The relaxation of the regime governing agencies is part of the explanation for the emergence of gangmasters in the past decade. In the absence of a licensing system, there is in practice great freedom for individuals to set up business as intermediaries and operate in whatever manner they see fit. The system of retrospective control contemplated by the rules on employment agencies is simply unsuited to the contemporary phenomenon of gangmasters – flexible, mobile and often operating at the margins of legality.

The inadequacy of the present arrangements as regards agencies is confirmed by the recent introduction of legislation on gangmasters. Pressure for the regulation of gangmasters had been building even before the Morecambe Bay tragedy of February 2004. That tragedy ensured parliamentary support for what became the Gangmasters Licensing Act 2004. The 2004 Act provides a framework for the regulation and supervision of the provision of labour in three sectors: agriculture, the gathering of shellfish, and food packing and processing. It defines a 'gangmaster' as anyone who supplies a worker to work for another in those sectors.[8] Crucially, the 2004 Act provides for a licensing system. Once the licensing system is operational, it will be a criminal offence to act as a gangmaster without a licence.[9] It will also be a criminal offence for an employer to arrange to be supplied with workers by an unlicensed gangmaster, save where 'reasonable steps' have been taken by the employer to ensure that the gangmaster has a valid licence.[10] Licensing is to be performed by the Gangmasters Licensing Authority, which came into operation on 1 April 2005. It is expected that the licensing system, with the criminal offences, will be in effect in mid-2006.[11]

The effects of the 2004 Act will to a large extent depend upon the details of the licensing system, and its enforcement. One concern which we have is with the proposal in the Hampton review of regulatory enforcement that the new Authority should be brought within the Health and Safety Executive.[12] The danger with such a development would be that it would undermine the specific function of regulating gangmasters which the 2004 Act sought to achieve.

We are also concerned that immigration and employment law enforcement should as far as possible be kept separate from one another in the operation of the Act. The government has indicated that its view is that "the issue of a licence will be dependent on a gangmaster demonstrating that his business is complying with general employment law (including immigration and taxation legislation)".[13] Our fear is that, if immigration and employment enforcement are merged in this way, even serious breaches of labour rights and standards will go unidentified, simply because individuals in an unauthorised position will be reluctant to come forward.

More generally, we would argue that the 2004 Act system is too cautious in its reintroduction of licensing of labour market intermediaries. The evidence of the past decade is that retrospective control on its own is inadequate to the task of preventing abusive practices by intermediaries. While this may be more of a problem in agriculture and related sectors, there is no reason why it should be limited to them. We would therefore favour the introduction of licensing of agencies and other intermediaries across the board.

b) *Who is the employer?*

A problem which often arises where workers are employed through a gangmaster or employment agency is that their employer is unclear. Are the workers employed by the intermediary, the user undertaking, or neither? The usual tests of employment status are whether there are mutual obligations to work and to pay for work done, and whether the organisation exercises control over the worker. In the case of agency workers, the legal outcome has generally been that the lack of control over work by the agency means that the worker and agency do not have an employment relationship. At the same time, there may be doubts as to whether the user undertaking is the employer, given that they are not responsible for payments. The difficulties in this area are illustrated by the 2004 Court of Appeal decision in the unfair dismissal case of *Brook Street Bureau v Dacas*.[14] The Court of Appeal found that an agency was not the employer of a cleaner they had provided to a local council for at least four years, even though the employment tribunal had earlier held that she had no contractual relationship with the local council.

With both gangmasters and agencies, it is critical that workers are able to identify an employer against whom they can enforce their rights. There are difficulties in either direction. Placing responsibility on the user organisation may be inconsistent with the fact that the more permanent relationship is with the intermediary, and that payments are made by it. Conversely, making the intermediary responsible is artificial where there is a long-term relationship with a user undertaking, and where the intermediary may disappear before claims against it can be enforced.

Our solution to these difficulties would be to treat the intermediary and the user undertaking as jointly liable, as employers, for compliance with the employment rights of their workers. This would maximise the protection available to workers. It would also have the advantage of obliging user undertakings to ensure the adequacy of the employment practices of intermediaries who supply them with labour, so as to avoid subsequent liability themselves.

c) Payments

The particular issue of payments to intermediaries should also be highlighted. In the United Kingdom it is unlawful for employment agencies to demand payment in return for the offer of employment.[15] Breach of this rule is a criminal offence for which the maximum fine is at present £5,000 (level 5). Nevertheless, recent research carried out in the East of England found many examples of agencies charging hundreds and sometimes thousands of pounds to migrant workers to secure them a job. This is not something which happens only to unauthorised workers: there is evidence for example of nurses employed from South East Asia being asked to pay large sums of money upfront to agencies in return for access to work. While these payments are said to represent travel and other arrangement costs, they are usually significantly higher than the cost of these services.[16]

In our view, the principle that workers should not have to pay intermediaries is a vital one. In order to affirm that principle in the context of migrant work, a number of steps are required. In the first place, it should be made explicit in legislation that any contract or arrangement for the payment of such fees, beyond the actual and documented cost of transport to the United Kingdom is unenforceable within the United Kingdom. Secondly, it should be made clear that the rules against charging by employment agencies based in the United Kingdom also apply in cases where they are involved in requests for such payments in other states. Finally, we would point out that compliance with this principle ought to be incorporated within the gangmasters licensing system – ie. evidence of payments should leave an individual open to the refusal or withdrawal of a licence.

2.3 Coverage

In considering the application of employment law to migrant workers, the question of coverage is of basic importance. Gaps or deficiencies in coverage are likely to have especially severe implications for migrant workers. Their employment patterns may not by typical of workers as whole, with the result that they fall outside of legal protections based on the typical employment relationship. The fact that migrant workers tend to be in a weaker labour market position than others is also relevant: the result is that employers will find it easier to take advantage of deficiencies in the legal framework in order to exclude migrant workers from legal entitlements.

A first problem as regards coverage concerns the application of employment law to workers other than employees. This category includes workers who, though technically self-employed, provide personal services under the direction of an employer. At present, some employment rights do apply to such workers: rights of non-discrimination, the minimum wage, protection against deductions, the regulation of working time and union membership rights. Other employment rights are however limited to employees, including the written statement of terms and conditions, the right to notice, protection against dismissal and redundancy, rights to maternity and parental leave, and the right to request flexible work arrangements. This difference of entitlement, dependent as it is on an individual's employment status, has been a source of criticism by trade unions, and is likely to work to the particular disadvantage of migrant workers. Our recommendation is that the government should use the power in section 23 of the Employment Relations Act 1999 in order to end the distinction between these two different contractual types. If this were to happen it would no longer be to employers' advantage to conclude contracts of service, instead of contracts of employment.

A second issue is that some employment rights are dependent on the length of service. For example, an employee with service under a year will not be able to enforce unfair dismissal or redundancy rights. Having legal rights based on length of service disadvantages migrant workers, who are more likely to have moved frequently from job to job and so have less opportunity to build up service entitlements. We recommend that there should be no service qualification for core employment rights as defined below.

3 Key employment rights

The focus of this chapter is on the application of key employment rights and labour standards to migrant workers. We identify the following rights as coming within the category, and discuss them in turn in this section:

- The right not to be discriminated against;
- The right to a written statement of employment terms;
- The right to enforce the contract of employment;
- The right to a pay statement;
- The right to the national minimum wage;
- The right not to have unlawful deductions from wages;
- The right to working time protection;
- The right to health and safety protection;
- The right to complain that dismissals or other employer decisions are unfair;
- The right to participate in union activities;
- The right to change employer;
- The right to social security.

3.1 Discrimination at work

United Kingdom employment legislation contains a code of anti-discrimination law, now covering a range of grounds including sex, disability, sexual orientation and religion or belief. The legislation which is of most immediate interest to migrant workers is the Race Relations Act 1976. In the employment sphere, as in other contexts, it prohibits discrimination on "racial grounds", which is defined to mean "colour, race, nationality or ethnic or national origins". This protection applies both to employees and workers. While the protection against discrimination appears comprehensive, complex issues arise from the particular status of the migrant worker.

There is abundant evidence from Citizens Advice Bureaux, trade unions and media reports of discrimination by employers against both legal and unauthorised migrant workers. In other words, the limitations of an individual's legal status or social situation in Britain is used as a reason to impose worse terms of employment and conditions of work than apply, or would apply, to workers with an unrestricted right of employment.

An important general question is therefore whether the definition of "racial grounds" in the 1976 Act is adequate to protect migrant workers. Our view is that it is not. In the first place, discrimination based on an individual's immigration status is quite distinct from discrimination against individuals of a given nationality. The term 'nationality' in the 1976 Act may have nothing to do with differences in immigration status: for example, discriminating against someone who is English, compared to the treatment of someone from Scotland would be unlawful. At the same time, employers who seek to take advantage of a worker's immigration status may well be indifferent as to the individual's specific nationality. This is by contrast with discrimination on grounds of nationality, which is more likely to be motivated by prejudice against particular groups than by an attempt to maximise the advantage to an employer of the vulnerability of an individual's position. In our view, the Race Relations Act ought therefore to be amended to include 'immigration status' as a further prohibited ground of discrimination, both in the employment sphere and beyond it.

We also propose the widening of the rule against harassment inserted into the Race Relations Act in 2003, in order to comply with EU Directive 2000/43 on discrimination on grounds of racial or ethnic origin. Harassment is defined as "violating [a] person's dignity" or "creating an intimidating, hostile, degrading, humiliating or offensive environment" for them. The rule against harassment does not however apply to the 'nationality' ground, let alone to immigration status. Our view is that, in order to strengthen the protection given to migrant workers, it should be applied to both. In cases where the discrimination amounts to abusive or threatening behaviour aimed at migrants, as opposed to non-migrants, we also recommend that compensation should include an amount representing an award for injury to feelings. Workers should have the right to bring such complaints not only against the employer but also against the individual responsible for the behaviour in question.

We do not underestimate the difficulties with the application of such a principle in practice. In particular, in the employment context, the lack of a comparator might make it difficult to prove what an employer would have done to a non-migrant. For that reason, our view is that some forms of conduct towards migrant workers ought to be automatically classified as breaches of the anti-discrimination principle. We would propose that the list should include as a minimum the following: failure to provide a statement of terms and conditions, the failure to provide an itemised pay statement, the failure to pay the minimum wage, the making of unauthorised deductions from wages and breaches of trade union rights.

3.2 A written statement of terms and conditions

Sections 1 and 2 of the Employment Rights Act 1996 give employees the right to a written statement of key employment terms. These include: the names of the employer and employee, the date the employment began, the rate of pay, the hours of work, any terms in relation to holidays or sickness, the job description, the employee's place of work and details of the employer's disciplinary and grievance procedures. The right covers all employees – ie. those working under a contract of employment.

The statement of terms and conditions is of particular significance for migrant workers. They are likely to have less information in general about employment rights and practices, so it is more important in their case that they should have access to documentary evidence of their contractual terms. If they do not have this, there is a greater danger in their case of employers failing to respect the terms on which they were hired, or the standard terms which were to have operated.

The obligation to provide a written statement is itself limited in key respects. Firstly, employers are allowed to provide the statement up to two months after the employee starts work. This seems to us too long a period in a situation where employment is temporary. In our view, a written statement of contract terms, in the migrant worker's own language or in a language that the migrant worker is literate in, should be provided either within one week, or by the first pay date, whichever is later in time. This would ensure that migrant workers are alerted to their employment entitlements. We propose a general amendment to s.1 of the Employment Rights Act to that effect.

Secondly, where an employer fails to provide a statement, the only remedy is an application to an employment tribunal for it to determine what the statement should have said. This seriously weakens the impact of the obligation to give a statement. In order to make the right to statement effective, our view is that it is necessary that there be compensation, paid to workers, in cases of non-compliance.

We further recommend that a failure to provide a migrant worker with a written statement of employment terms should amount to an act of immigration status discrimination, with rights to compensation calculated on the basis of discrimination law, including the right to compensation for injury to feelings.

3.3 The contract of employment

A particular problem which can face migrant workers is that they are promised certain terms and conditions in order to persuade them to come to Britain, only to find on arrival that these are not in fact on offer. A report by the Citizens' Advice Bureaux found that agencies often make attractive but misleading promises to recruit workers from their home countries.[17] These may relate for example to the work to be done, the wages, and accommodation arrangements.

In our view, where migrant workers have documentary evidence that they have been promised certain terms and conditions, these should be deemed to form part of the contract of employment or contract for services. Thereafter, migrant workers should be protected against unilateral changes to the contract by the employer. There may of course be cases where changes in circumstances occur between the

> ## False promises
>
> Y, a qualified nurse, was recruited through an agency to work in the United Kingdom. She was told that there were good opportunities here and that the pay would be high. She paid the agency £2,500 for what she was told was the cost of a work permit. She was not given a job as a nurse, but instead works as a care assistant doing a 58-60 hour week. She is paid just a little above the national minimum – £5.36 an hour – but there is no overtime rate even though she works so many hours
>
> She has tried to take an adaptation course to be registered as a nurse in England but despite having written to nearly 50 hospitals she has not been able to get on a course.
>
> *Source: Working Lives Research Institute, East of England project 2005*

initial description of the job and the date on which the individual starts working. This could arise in particular where a significant period has elapsed between the two events. In such cases we recommend that any variation to the original offer of terms should not be permitted within the first three months of employment, so as to provide the migrant worker with a guaranteed period of stability. In cases where it transpires that the work as described is not available, we recommend that the worker should be given the option to work in the alternative but with compensation to reflect the value of the original post as described, for a three month period. Alternatively, where the worker chooses not to accept the alternative work, we recommend that the employer or agency should be obliged to compensate the worker, to reflect the value of the promised post over a three-month period.

3.4 Itemised pay statements

Section 8 of the Employment Rights Act 1996 provides that every employee, by their first pay date, must be given an itemised pay statement that lists gross wages, deductions and net wages. Ensuring the effectiveness of the entitlement to a pay statement is – as with the statement of terms and conditions – of critical importance in the case of migrant workers. In general, their relative unfamiliarity with British systems of labour law, national insurance and tax means that they more than other workers require accurate information as to how much they are paid, and what deductions have been made. It is also important for migrant workers to have documentary evidence of having paid national insurance contributions and income tax. Otherwise migrant workers may believe that these deductions are being made, even though in reality the amounts are never forwarded to the State authorities. If the worker has a pay statement, the issue then becomes one of the State authorities pursing the employer for non-payment.

We also call attention to the weakness of the remedy where an employer fails to provide an itemised pay statement. At present, the only possibility is for workers to obtain a declaration from an employment tribunal that a statement has not been given, as to its correct content. Here too, our view is that in order to make the right to an itemised pay statement effective, compensation, paid to workers, should be required in cases of non-compliance. In addition, we recommend that a failure to provide a migrant worker with a pay statement be treated as action taken against the worker on the grounds of immigration status, with rights to compensation calculated on the basis of discrimination law, including the right to compensation for injury to feelings.

3.5 The national minimum wage

Under the National Minimum Wage Act 1998 all workers in the United Kingdom – and not just employees – have the right to a minimum wage. The wage is set at different levels, depending on the worker's age and on whether they are undergoing training. The basic amounts, effective from 1 October 2005, are £5.05 an hour for those aged 22 or over, £4.25 an hour for those aged 18 to 21 and £3 an hour for 16 and 17 year olds. The minimum is subject to deductions for national insurance and income tax. There is also a specific minimum wage in agriculture, which since 1 October 2004 has been £5.40 an hour for most adult workers. Both the general and the agricultural minimum wages are enforced by the Inland Revenue, using powers given by the National Minimum Wage Act 1998.

There is evidence of employers not paying migrant workers the minimum wages, to which they are entitled. In recent research conducted in the East of England, migrant workers – both documented and undocumented – were being paid below the national minimum wage. It seems likely that the concentration of migrant workers in lower paid employment, and their greater vulnerability to employers, means that the failure to respect the minimum wage is a particularly acute problem for them.[18]

In our view, the main weakness of the minimum wage system is the limited penalties for employer non-compliance. As the Low Pay Commission put it in its most recent report on the national minimum wage:

"It is apparent that most employers who do not pay the minimum wage and have enforcement action taken against them are no worse off than if they had paid the minimum wage at the outset. Indeed, in many cases they may even be better off as they are not required to pay interest on underpayment of arrears to the worker. Nor is there any other financial penalty imposed for late payment in itself, except in cases where a penalty notice has been issued (although the financial penalty is not paid to the worker concerned). A worker, however, who is paid below the minimum wage is likely to suffer financial hardship even if arrears are eventually paid, since they do not receive interest to reflect the later payment."[19]

We agree with the Low Pay Commission's proposals that legislation should provide for the payment of interest on arrears, and financial penalties for seriously non-compliant employers.[20]

We would however go further and suggest a strengthening of penalties in several respects. In the first place, there should be a penalty element in all cases of non-compliance. At present, the initial remedy is an 'enforcement order', which merely instructs the employer to pay the monies owed. It is only if that is not complied with that a 'penalty order' is imposed, set at twice the minimum wage rate for every day of non-compliance with the enforcement order. Secondly, we suggest a departure from the present position, so as to pay all penalties to the workers in question, since that would provide an incentive to their bringing of complaints. Thirdly, where employers or agencies fail to pay migrant workers at the appropriate national minimum wage rate, we would argue that that be treated as a case of immigration status discrimination, since it would necessarily amount to an act taken against them due to their labour market position as migrant workers. Such a failure to pay the national minimum rate to migrant workers should give rise to a right to compensation calculated on the basis of discrimination law, including the right to compensation for injury to feelings.

A final issue which we would highlight in this area concerns the specific case of unauthorised workers. The Low Pay Commission's most recent report records the intention that, where the Inland Revenue finds evidence of unauthorised working, it will share this information with the Home Office.[21] We are not convinced that this is a wise approach to take. Fear that the Inland Revenue will pass on information in this way can only serve to seriously hamper the identification of employers who are failing to pay the minimum wage.

3.6 Deductions from wages

Deductions from wages were previously regulated by the Truck Acts 1831-1940, which were among the earliest examples of worker protection through legislation. These Acts sought to ensure that workers were paid in money rather than in goods and services. They also limited the deductions which could be made from manual workers to those which had been authorised by the worker's contract, were "fair and reasonable" and related to the employer's loss. By the mid-1980s the then Conservative government argued that the legislation

> ## Deductions
> Interviews carried out in the East of England found that workers earning just the national minimum wage had deductions for transport (£2 to £3 a day), uniforms (£10 to £30 a time) and accommodation (anything between £25 and £100 a week for shared accommodation). In one case an Eastern European woman working in agriculture was paying more than £70 a week for a space in a communal tent which in peak season could accommodate 200 workers.
>
> *Source: Working Lives Research Institute, East of England project 2005*

was anachronistic and that payments in kind were no longer an issue of concern. They therefore secured the repeal of the Truck Acts, and replaced them with the Wages Act 1986, which became Part 11 of the Employment Rights Act 1996. Part 11 sets down rules regarding deductions from pay. Crucially, these do not limit the amounts that can be deducted (other than for retail workers), provided the grounds for the deduction have been agreed in writing in advance.

Deductions are also largely permitted under the legislation on the minimum wage. Sums deducted which arise out of a worker's conduct, or which relate to goods and services provided to a worker, nevertheless count towards the minimum wage. Employers are also permitted to make deductions for accommodation (known as the 'accommodation offset') up to a maximum of £3.75 per day.

There is evidence that migrant workers are particularly vulnerable to excessive deductions from pay. Reports from CAB offices show that migrant workers often face large deductions for items like uniforms, transport and accommodation. Workers may also have deductions made from their wages for 'poor' work or other alleged failures in employment. Where these practices occur, workers may end up being paid less then the minimum wage, and may indeed end up with little or no cash income.[22]

What this evidence shows is that the current permissive regime as regards deductions opens the door to the non-payment of workers, and particularly migrant workers. In our view, what is required is the introduction of a new 'Truck Act' to regulate both the payment of wages and deductions. It should be unlawful for employers to provide goods and services as an alternative to wages, and also impermissible for employers to make deductions from wages for goods and services provided. It should also be unlawful for an employer to make deductions from pay, other than permitted deductions for accommodation, where the effect would be to reduce the worker's gross earnings to less than the national minimum wage.

The provision of accommodation by employers raises special issues.

Here too, there is evidence from Citizens' Advice Bureaux that migrant workers often face accommodation deductions which are significant relative to wages, even for accommodation which is over-crowded and substandard.[23] Our solution would be to generalise the 'accommodation offset' in the minimum wage legislation, so that it would be a maximum for accommodation deductions in all cases. We would also argue that, in order to address the question of the quality of accommodation, employers should not be able to make any deduction at all from a worker's pay where the accommodation offered is multi-occupancy (meaning that individuals do not have their own room).

3.7 Working time

The legal regulation of working time in Britain, under the Working Time Regulations 1998, is highly limited. The maximum average working week is 48 hours, and anyway employers can lawfully ask their workers to 'opt out' of even that protection. This legal position is particularly damaging with respect to migrant workers. There is evidence that many migrant workers are working long hours and doing shift work. Interviews with CAB workers show many migrants working unsociable shifts and then taking it in turns to sleep. Long shift patterns are common in sectors like the food processing industry.[24] Migrant workers may be particularly vulnerable to long hours and shift work, where they are trying to earn as much as possible to enable them to send remittances home while maintaining themselves in this country.

It is obvious that migrant workers should have the same protection as United Kingdom workers in relation to working time. We are concerned however that the particular vulnerability of migrant workers, and the fact that they may not understand any documentation they are asked to sign, means that they may agree to opt out of the 48 hour work without fully understanding what is involved or what their entitlements are. Our proposal to protect migrant workers is that an individual opt-out should not be valid unless it is attached to a document in the worker's mother tongue, or a language which the worker is literate in, which informs the worker of the right to opt into the 48-hour week without penalty.

In other publications the Institute of Employment Rights has stressed the need for reform of the law relating to working time, and in particular for an end to the individual opt-out from the 48 hour maximum average working week.[25] We support this position in general, since migrant workers are especially likely to be required to work long hours by their employers. Special considerations apply however to migrant workers on seasonal schemes, where it is necessary to ensure that restrictions on the weekly working time do not limit their earning capacity. In their case, we favour a lengthy reference period for the 48 hour week. The present position, whereby the reference period in seasonal activities is 26 weeks, rather than 17 weeks, appears to us an acceptable compromise in this regard.

We would also call attention to a specific issue concerning parental rights with respect to working time. Rights to parental leave, to time off in a family emergency, and to request flexible working to care for children do not appear to extend to situations where the child does not reside in the United Kingdom. This is an example of a possible way in which migrant workers may lose out on employment rights. In our view, the relevant legislation should be clarified to ensure that children outside the United Kingdom are covered by these rights.

3.8 Health and safety

There are several reasons why migrant workers face greater health and safety risks than the working population as a whole. They are more likely to engage in work which is undesirable and dangerous. If they are employed through agencies and gangmasters, neither the intermediary nor the user employer may give them adequate training. Their background may mean that they lack experience or training in the use of certain machinery and equipment. They may anyway face extra health and safety risks as a result of insufficient knowledge of English or the fact that a workforce consists of individuals who speak different languages: this will both affect the training they receive and limit the communication of information about imminent risks.

For these reasons, additional strategies are needed to deliver a safe working environment to migrant workers and in the workplaces where they work. In the first place, it is necessary for employers to take into account the circumstances of migrant workers. This can be seen in the decision of the Court of Appeal in the case of *Tasci v Pekalp*.[26] It concerned a Kurdish refugee who had apparently exaggerated his woodworking competence in order to obtain employment, and then suffered a serious injury to his hand after three weeks working with a circular saw. The court set out in the following terms what it took to be the duty of an employer to provide adequate training in such a case:

"Here, [the] applicant was a refugee from a remote part of Eastern Europe. Any prudent employer would have recognised the high probability that he could put little or no reliance upon any representations made by the applicant for work as to his previous experience and training, on the basis that a person seeking refugee status would be prepared to say almost anything in the desperate need to obtain employment to support himself in this country. In any event, the standards of training and education that obtain in woodworking establishments in Eastern Turkey may bear little or no relation to the standards that apply in this country. In truth, the prudent employer, faced with the problems that this applicant for work would have presented, would have treated him as a total novice and have started, ab initio, with a training and supervision regime in order to satisfy himself that his new worker was capable of operating a circular saw safely."

In our view, the implication of *Tasci v Pekalp* is that employers have a duty to allow for the particular circumstances of migrant workers when it comes to fulfilling their health and safety obligations.

The language in which health and safety information and training is provided is a second issue. It is self-evident that, where employers hire migrant workers whose English is not fluent, the fulfilment of health and safety obligations requires communication in a language the workers understand. In our opinion, there should be a statutory duty on employers who hire workers whose mother tongue is not English to communicate health and safety information in a language in which the workers are literate.

Finally, we would propose that the supervision mechanisms with respect to health and safety should seek to take into account the special position of migrant workers. Employers should be required to monitor and report separately to the Health and Safety Executive on the size of their migrant workforce, and on health and safety issues relevant to them. In addition, the Health and Safety Executive should have a duty to inspect workplaces at regular intervals (such as six months) where there are ten or more workers who were born outside the United Kingdom and who have been in the United Kingdom for fewer than five years.

3.9 Dismissals and other employer decisions

There are a number of distinct issues for migrant workers who wish to challenge dismissals or other adverse employer decisions. The first of these concerns the statutory procedures introduced on 1 October 2004 for dismissals, disciplinary decisions and employees' grievances.[27] Since compliance or non-compliance with these procedures will in most cases affect the outcome of any subsequent employment tribunal proceedings, it is vital that employees are aware of them. In practice, limited information on employment rights and company internal procedures and a limited knowledge of English may disproportionately disadvantage migrant workers. For that reason, we recommend that employers be obliged to provide copies of contractual grievance procedures or the statutory grievance procedure to workers in a language in which the workers are literate. A related issue concerns the statutory requirement that dismissal, disciplinary and grievance procedures be conducted in a manner that enables the employee to explain their case. In our view, this provision should be clarified to entitle a worker who is not fluent in English to an interpreter and translation.

A second issue concerns the position of unauthorised workers who are dismissed. As indicated in section 2, above, we take the view that unauthorised workers should in general be permitted to assert employment rights, including rights in relation to dismissal. There is however a difficulty that there are penalties on an employer who employs someone who is not authorised to work. Our opposition to those penalties is set out in chapter 4. In this context, the question arises whether an employer should be free to dismiss a worker whom they discover to be unauthorised. In the current state of the law, even if the doctrine of illegality (discussed in section 2) did not in general apply, an employer could argue that 'illegality' was a potentially fair reason for the dismissal. We submit that this situation is undesirable to the extent that it does not afford the employee the opportunity to clarify or regularise their immigration and consequent employment status. We therefore propose that, in such a situation, a worker should be afforded a period of three months' grace prior to a dismissal's coming into force, in order for them to clarify or regularise their position. If they are able to demonstrate or obtain permission to work, they should then have the right to seek re-instatement or re-engagement. An unreasonable refusal by the employer to re-instate or re-engage would amount to an act of immigration status discrimination, giving a right to compensation calculated on the basis of discrimination law.

A final question in this area concerns the dismissal of migrant workers where they complain about their treatment by an employer, or employment conditions more generally. The reason this is of particular concern for migrant workers is that they may be especially dependent on remaining in employment. As we saw in chapter three, regular migrants are restricted in their right to change employer, their immigration status may depend on their remaining in employment, and they may be unable to claim benefits during periods when they are out of work. The risks of loss of employment for unauthorised workers are even greater, given their inherently marginalised place in society and the labour market.

As the law stands, it is automatically unfair to dismiss an employee in several circumstances: where they raise a health and safety matter in an employment where there is no safety representative, where they assert a statutory employment right, or where action is taken to enforce the minimum wage.[28] The problem with the current law is that it does nothing for persons who complain about their treatment at work – for example, a failure to pay agreed wages – without a specific statutory right being involved. This is particularly problematic for migrant workers, because of their weaker position within the workforce. In our view, it should also be automatically unfair to dismiss a worker who raises a grievance with an employer.

In order to protect migrant workers, it is also necessary to guarantee their immigration position where they make legitimate complaints. For regular workers, our view is that this difficulty should be addressed by allowing them to change employer and to claim social benefits. While the position of unauthorised workers is undoubtedly more complex, we would argue that, where an employment-related claim has been presented, a migrant worker should be permitted to remain on the territory, take alternative employment, and claim social benefits until the claim has been disposed of.

3.10 Trade union rights

Migrant workers are more likely than other workers to need the support of trade unions precisely because they are often in a position of vulnerability. The employment rights covered in this chapter are only effective if migrant workers can enforce them. At the same time, workers acting on their own typically find it difficult to resist the kinds of exploitative employer practices discussed here. There is also a range of particular services which trade unions can usefully provide to migrant workers, including interpretation and translation facilities for key employment documents, the provision of literature on employment rights in the migrant workers' language, representation in dismissal, disciplinary and grievance procedures and assistance in cases where they are being unfairly treated by gangmasters and agencies.

These considerations point to the importance of trade union organisation to migrant workers, and to the need for public policy to actively encourage their union membership. One change we would propose concerns the protections in the Trade Union and Labour Relations (Consolidation) Act 1992 against victimisation and dismissal on the grounds of trade union membership or the taking of industrial action. In order to reflect the particular position of migrant workers, we would recommend a strengthening of this protection in their case. Where a migrant worker is victimised by an employer for having joined or taken part in a trade union or industrial action, this should also be treated as a breach of the law on discrimination on grounds of immigration status, discussed above.

Beyond that, the particular vulnerability of migrant workers points to the need for trade unions to be given autonomous rights within labour law. This is a subject on which proposals have been made in previous Institute of Employment Rights publications.[29] We would highlight in particular the importance of union access to a workforce with a view to recruitment: this is especially needed because migrant workers are likely to be unfamiliar with the operation of trade unions and labour relations in Britain. We would also highlight the need for unions to have rights to enforce employment laws independently of workers, in circumstances where individual workers do not wish to come forward for fear of an employer response, or simply do not wish themselves to pursue a complaint.

3.11 The freedom to change employer

The possibility to change employer is a basic principle in a labour market. Just as other workers do, migrant workers may want to leave one employer and find work with another for a variety of reasons. There may be social and personal reasons for the change. They may expect better conditions, or more interesting work. Or they may be unhappy at their treatment by the first employer and simply wish to resign.

The significance of the right of migrant workers to change employer was considered in chapter three, and we recommended that there should be far greater possibilities for migrant workers to change employers than at present. That is not however the only issue which arises here. There is evidence that some migrant workers are effectively prevented from leaving their employer by a variety of practices such as the retention of their identity documents, or of a form of bonds which the employer withholds if a worker leaves. These practices amount to a situation of forced labour.

In order to address these practices, we believe that the intervention of the criminal law is necessary. It should be a criminal offence for an employer, agency or other body to retain a worker's identity documents without their consent. It should also be a criminal offence for any employer to require a bond from an employee against future performance or employment. We also recommend that where workers allege that their documents have been taken from them and that they have not been issued with a contract, they should have the legal right to seek alternative employment, regardless of their immigration status.

3.12 Social security

We considered the question of the entitlement of migrant workers to non-contributory benefits in chapter three. We have one further recommendation in relation to benefits which depended upon employer involvement, which concerns the payment of statutory sick pay and statutory maternity pay benefits through an employer. We recommend that there be a legal obligation on the employer to inform migrant workers, in their mother tongue, or in a language in which the workers are literate, of the existence of the benefits and how to claim them.

3.13 Information about employment rights

A final, general point in relation to employment rights concerns the provision of information. The unfamiliarity of migrant workers with employment law and sources of support in the United Kingdom makes it critical that they have accurate and accessible information about employment rights. The first stage is the provision of information to migrant workers before they come to Britain, or on arrival. The Department of Trade and Industry currently has documents of this nature in Lithuanian, Polish and Portuguese, which were produced in co-operation with the governments of the respective countries.[30] In addition, when workers from the A8 accession states register under the Workers' Registration Scheme (see chapter three), they receive an English language leaflet produced by the TUC entitled *Starting to work in the UK*.[31] While these initiatives are clearly to be welcomed, we would argue that more could be done. The objective should be to ensure that *all* migrant workers who register with the immigration authorities receive information, both in English and in their own language, as to their legal entitlements. This should be achieved in co-operation with the TUC.

It is also important that migrant workers have information available to them if they wish to complain about their treatment by an employer. In our view, the main public bodies concerned with labour law should endeavour to provide at least basic information in the major languages of migrant workers. This includes the Employment Tribunal Service, the Health and Safety Executive and ACAS. These bodies should also have a duty to ensure that, where migrant workers lack fluency in English, they should be able to proceed with a complaint in their own language.

4 Conclusion

In this chapter, we have shown that the presence of significant numbers of migrant workers in the British labour force calls for basic changes to employment law. In the first place, what is required is to take seriously the principle that migrant workers should not be discriminated against. That principle implies that unauthorised workers should not be excluded from the protection of employment law, that discrimination law should include immigration status as a prohibited ground of differentiation among workers, and that certain forms of employer conduct to migrant workers should be classed as inherently discriminatory. It also implies that the special position of migrant workers be reflected in employment law – for example, through linguistic requirements on employers and government agencies, or through the introduction of a specific offence of withholding travel documents.

The argument of this chapter goes much wider than that, however. Many of the abusive practices now faced primarily by migrant workers – such as the power of intermediaries, the non-issuing of statements, the non-payment of the minimum wage, unlawful deductions from wages, dangerous workplaces and excessive working hours – are not specific to migrant workers. They are rather the end result of processes of deregulation in the labour market, and the related casualisation of the labour force, particularly in lower paid sectors and occupations. If we are to improve the position of migrant workers, what is needed is a renewed acceptance of the need for labour market regulation for all workers. This is the powerful message which emerges from the close examination of the position of migrant workers within employment law.

Notes

1 [1995] ECR 1091.
2 [2004] 4 All ER 1056, [2005] ICR 231.
3 [2001] ICR 99.
4 ILO Committee on Freedom of Association, rulings against Spain (Report 327 on complaint by UGT, 2002) and the USA (Report 332 on complaint by AFL-CIO and CTM, 2003).
5 See House of Commons Environment, Food and Rural Affairs Select Committee, *Gangmasters*, 8th Report, Session 2003-04, Recommendations 1-3.
6 SI 2003 No. 3319.
7 Employment Agencies Act 1973, sections 13(2) and 13(3).
8 Gangmasters Licensing Act 2004, section 4.
9 Gangmasters Licensing Act 2004, sections 6 and 12.
10 Gangmasters Licensing Act 2004, section 13.
11 Written statement by Minister for Environment, Food and Rural Affairs, Alun Michael, *House of Commons Debates*, 4 March 2005.
12 HM Treasury, *Reducing Administrative Burdens: Effective Inspection and Enforcement* (March 2005), p 65.
13 *Explanatory Memorandum to the Draft Gangmasters (Licensing Authority) Regulations* 2005, para 7.2.
14 [2004] IRLR 358.
15 Employment Agencies Act 1973, section 6.
16 S McKay and A Winklemann-Gleed, *Migrant Workers in the East of England* (London: East of England Development Agency, 2005, forthcoming).
17 Citizens Advice Bureaux, *Nowhere to Turn: CAB Evidence on the Exploitation of Migrant Workers* (London, 2004), p 6.
18 McKay and Winklemann-Gleed, forthcoming.
19 Department of Trade and Industry, *National Minimum Wage: Low Pay Commission Report 2005*, Cm 6475, February 2005), para 6.46.
20 Ibid, para 6.48.
21 Ibid, para 6.20.
22 Citizens Advice Bureaux, pp 13-14.
23 Ibid, p 6.
24 McKay and Winklemann-Gleed, forthcoming.
25 K Ewing and J Hendy (eds), *A Charter of Workers' Rights* (London: Institute of Employment Rights, 2002), p 38.
26 [2001] ICR 633.
27 The Employment Act 2002 (Dispute Resolution) Regulations 2004, SI 2004 No 752.
28 Employment Rights Act 1996, sections 100, 104 and 104A.
29 See in particular, K Ewing, S Moore and S Wood, *Unfair Labour Practices: trade union recognition and employer resistance* (London: Institute of Employment Rights, 2003).
30 Further details can be found at:
   http://www.dti.gov.uk/er/agency/migrant_workers.htm.
31 The text of the leaflet can be found at:
   http://www.tuc.org.uk/international/tuc-7982-f0.cfm#tuc-7982-3.

Chapter 6

International agreements on labour migration

1 Introduction

The field of labour migration is an especially suitable one for international action. Migrant workers' states of nationality have a legitimate interest in ensuring the fairness of the treatment of their nationals who live and work elsewhere. Many of the expectations as to what fair treatment entails have now been codified by international treaties on migrant workers. These international norms are also sustained by the need to avoid 'unfair competition' among states of destination, who have an interest in avoiding one another's exploitative treatment of migrant workers.

This chapter provides a summary of the main international treaties and other texts which lay down standards for the treatment of migrant workers. These are organised according to the source of the instruments and texts in question: the International Labour Organisation (ILO), the Council of Europe and the United Nations. We also consider important recent decisions of the Inter-American Court of Human Rights and the ILO Committee on Freedom of Association on the specific question of the treatment of unauthorised workers.

2 ILO instruments

The ILO has adopted two main Conventions which deal with the rights of migrant workers: the Migration for Employment Convention (ILO Convention 97, 1949) and the Migrant Workers (Supplementary Provisions) Convention (ILO Convention 143, 1975). The application of the provisions of these conventions is limited to the nationals of the states party to them, and to refugees and stateless persons that are resident in those states.

In addition to these Conventions, the ILO has also produced non-binding recommendations related to the rights of migrant workers and their families. These are the Migration for Employment Recommendation (ILO Recommendation 86 of 1949) and the Migrant Workers Recommendation (ILO Recommendation 151 of 1975). These recommendations both explain and amplify the standards contained in the conventions.

2.1 Migration for Employment Convention 1949

The core principle of Convention 97 is that all migrant workers should receive the same treatment as nationals with regard to terms and conditions of employment and working conditions. Under Article 6 of Convention 97, equal treatment is required, among other matters, in relation to remuneration, hours of work, holidays, membership of a trade union, collective bargaining, social security and taxation.

Article 2 of the Convention requires contracting states "to maintain, or satisfy itself that there is maintained, an adequate and free service to assist migrants for employment, and in particular to provide them with accurate information".

Convention 97 by contrast offers only limited protection with respect to immigration policy. Article 8 provides that workers who have been admitted on a permanent basis, and their family members, may not be returned to their state of origin if they become incapacitated due to illness or injury. This right can however be suspended until five years' residence, and can anyway be limited by international agreement with the state of origin. No provision is made in Convention 97 for the immigration entitlements of family members, or for the security of residence of migrant workers in other circumstances.

Convention 97 has been ratified by 43 states, including the United Kingdom. We recommend that a formal review be undertaken to ensure the compatibility of United Kingdom law and policy with its requirements.

2.2 Migration for Employment Recommendation 1949

Convention 97 is supplemented by Recommendation 86, adopted on the same day. Paragraph 4 provides that it should be a general policy of contracting states to develop and utilise all possibilities of employment. For this purpose, contracting states should facilitate the international distribution of manpower and, in particular, the movement of manpower from countries which have a surplus of manpower to those that have a deficiency.

Paragraph 5 of the Recommendation gives greater detail in relation to the free assistance service to be given to migrant workers by virtue of Article 2 of Convention 97. This service should advise migrants and their families, in their languages or in a language they can understand, on matters relating to emigration, immigration, employment and living conditions, including health conditions in the place of destination. Paragraph 5 further states that preparatory courses should be provided to inform migrants of the general conditions and methods of work prevailing in the country of immigration, and to instruct them in the language of that country. The countries of emigration and immigration should co-operate in organising such courses.

According to Paragraph 8 of the Recommendation, there should be a reasonable interval between the publication and the coming into force of any measure altering the conditions on which immigration or the employment of migrants is permitted.

Paragraph 10 states that migrants for employment should be provided in cases of necessity with adequate accommodation, food and clothing on arrival in the country of immigration. Migration should also be facilitated by ensuring, where necessary, vocational training in order to enable the migrants for employment to acquire the qualifications required in the country of immigration.

In relation to family reunification, Paragraph 15 states that agreement should be reached authorising migrants for employment on a permanent basis to be accompanied or joined by the members of their family.

Paragraph 16 provides that migrants for employment authorised to reside in a territory and the members of their families authorised to accompany or join them should, as far as possible, be admitted to employment on the same conditions as nationals. Where such restrictions exist, they should cease within five years of a migrant residing regularly in the country.

Since Recommendation 86 is intended to supplement Convention 97, which the United Kingdom has ratified, we recommend a formal review of the compatibility of United Kingdom policy with its provisions.

2.3 Migrant Workers (Supplementary Provisions) Convention 1975

Article 10 of Convention 143 contains a similar guarantee of equal treatment to that in Convention 97. Under Article 10, contracting states are under an obligation to promote and guarantee equality of opportunity and treatment, among other things, in respect of employment and occupation, social security and membership of and participation in trade unions.

Convention 143 goes further than Convention 97 by making provision for changes of employer. Article 8 sets out the proposition that workers who have "resided legally in the territory for the purpose of employment" should not become unauthorised simply through loss of employment. Accordingly, they are to be given equality of treatment with nationals as regards security of employment, alternative employment and retraining. Article 14(a) contains a more general provision for the free choice of employment for migrant workers. It states that a contracting state can:

"Make the free choice of employment, while assuring migrant workers the right to geographical mobility, subject to the conditions that the migrant worker has resided lawfully within its territory for the purpose of employment for a prescribed period not exceeding two years or, if its laws or regulations provide for contracts for a fixed term of less than two years, that the worker has completed his first work contract."

Two years is therefore the maximum period for which restrictions may be imposed.

Unauthorised workers are specifically protected by Convention 143 in one respect. Article 9 provides that where a worker is unauthorised, and cannot have their situation regularised, they and their families should nevertheless, "enjoy equality of treatment... in respect of rights arising out of past employment as regards remuneration, social security and other benefits."

Convention 143 contains only limited provision for the right of family reunion. Article 13(1) of Convention 143 merely provides that States "may take all necessary measures to facilitate the reunification of the families of all migrant workers residing in their territory". It goes on to define the family for these purposes as "the spouse and dependent children, father and mother".

In addition to laying down these standards, Part I of Convention 143 covers policies against unauthorised employment. In particular, Article 3 provides that contracting states "shall adopt all necessary and appropriate measures, both within its jurisdiction and in collaboration with other [states]" in order to "suppress clandestine movements of migrants for employment and illegal employment of migrants". This obligation includes action against "the organisers of illicit or clandestine movements of migrants for employment departing from, passing through or arriving in its territory", and "against those who employ workers who have immigrated in illegal conditions".

Convention 143 has been ratified by 18 states. These do not include the United Kingdom, but do include five EU member States: Cyprus, Italy, Portugal, Slovenia and Sweden. We are in favour of the minimum standards as to the treatment of migrant workers which the Convention contains. We note however that the Convention's Article 3 is inconsistent with our opposition to the imposition of penalties on employers of unauthorised workers (see chapter four, above). For that reason, rather than recommend that the United Kingdom ratify Convention 143, we propose a formal review of United Kingdom immigration policy for compliance with the minimum standards of protection for migrant workers set out in the Convention.

2.4 Migrant Workers Recommendation 1975

Recommendation 151 was adopted on the same day as Convention 143, and gives greater detail to it and to Convention 97. Paragraph 2 of the Recommendation elaborates the principle of equal treatment. It includes the following among the matters in respect of which migrant workers and members of their families should enjoy effective equality of opportunity and treatment with nationals of the state concerned:

- Access to vocational guidance
- Access to vocational training and employment
- Security of employment, the provision of alternative employment and retraining
- Remuneration for work of equal value
- Conditions of work, including hours of work, rest periods, annual holidays with pay, occupational safety and occupational health measures
- Social security measures and welfare facilities and benefits provided in connection with employment
- Membership of trade unions, exercise of trade union rights and eligibility for office in trade unions and in labour-management relations bodies, including bodies representing workers in undertakings
- Housing and the benefits of social services and educational and health facilities.

Paragraph 7 sets out the measures that the State should take to ensure migrant workers and their families can take full advantage of their rights and opportunities in employment and occupation. These include:

- The provision of information to migrant workers, as far as possible in their mother tongue or, if that is not possible, in a language with which they are familiar, of their rights under national law and practice as regards the matters in Paragraph 2
- Measures to advance their knowledge of the language or languages of the country of employment, as far as possible during paid time.

Here too, we recommend a formal review of the compatibility of United Kingdom policy with the standards set out in ILO Recommendation 151.

3 Council of Europe instruments

There are a number of Council of Europe instruments which are relevant to the position of migrant workers. The summary here focuses on instruments which the United Kingdom has ratified. Becuase of its subject matter, this section also covers the Council of Europe Convention on Migrant Workers of 1977, even though it has not been ratified by the United Kingdom.

3.1 European Convention on Human Rights 1950

The ECHR is applicable to all individuals residing in those countries which have ratified it, and not merely to nationals of other contracting States. In accordance with Article 1 of the Convention, the ratifying States shall secure to "everyone within their jurisdiction the rights and freedoms" defined in the Convention. Article 4 contains a prohibition on slavery and forced labour which is of relevance in the case of unauthorised work. Article 8, on the right to private and family life, is of relevance to migrant workers because it is a potential source of immigration entitlements for family members. Also relevant are Articles 10 and 11, which guarantee the rights to freedom of expression and peaceful assembly and association. In addition, Article 14 guarantees non-discrimination in the enjoyment of the rights and freedoms protected under the Convention, "on any ground such as sex, race, colour, language, religion, political or other opinion, national or social origin, association with a national minority, property, birth or other status." The United Kingdom has both ratified the ECHR and given it effect in domestic law though the Human Rights Act 1998.

Reference may also be made here to Protocol 12 of the ECHR, which was signed in 2000 and came into force on 1 April 2005. It prohibits discrimination in the enjoyment of all of the rights contained in the law of the ratifying State. Its Article 1 provides that "The enjoyment of any right set forth by law shall be secured without discrimination on any ground such as sex, race, colour, language, religion, political or other opinion, national or social origin, association with a national minority, property, birth or other status." We call on the United Kingdom to ratify Protocol 12, particularly because of its potential application to the position of migrant workers.

3.2 European Convention on Social and Medical Assistance 1953

The European Convention on Social and Medical Assistance confers entitlements to social and medical assistance, and protects migrants who are or may become dependent upon such assistance. Its Article 1 sets out the principle of access to social assistance, for nationals of other contracting parties, in the following terms:

"Each of the Contracting Parties undertakes to ensure that nationals of the other Contracting Parties who are lawfully present in any part of its territory to which this Convention applies, and who are without sufficient resources, shall be entitled equally with its own nationals and on the same conditions to social and medical assistance... provided by the legislation in force from time to time in that part of its territory."

Article 6 of the Convention expressly precludes the repatriation of nationals of Contracting Parties who are lawfully resident "on the sole ground that [they are] in need of assistance".

The United Kingdom is one of 18 states to have ratified the Convention on Social and Medical Assistance. There is one non-EEA contracting state, which is Turkey. Given the limits to social benefits for non-EEA nationals (discussed in section 7.2 of chapter three, above), we recommend a review of the compatibility of British policy with this Convention and changes to policy if it is found not to be compliant.

3.3 European Convention on Establishment 1955

The European Convention on Establishment is intended to encourage long-term residence by Council of Europe nationals in the territory of other states. Article 10 of the Convention gives a right to engage in a "gainful occupation" in other contracting states:

"Each Contracting Party shall authorise nationals of the other Parties to engage in its territory in any gainful occupation on an equal footing with its own nationals, unless the said Contracting Party has cogent economic or social reasons for withholding the authorisation. This provision shall apply, but not be limited, to industrial, commercial, financial and agricultural occupations, skilled crafts and the professions, whether the person concerned is self-employed or is in the service of an employer."

Article 12 then provides for a general right to engage in "any gainful occupation", without being subject to Article 10 restrictions, for three categories of person: those who have been "lawfully engaged in any gainful occupation" for five years, those who have been lawfully resident for 10 years, and anyone admitted to permanent residence. The United Kingdom policies on the employment of settled persons (discussed in chapter three, above) and on the acquisition of settlement through long residence (discussed in chapter four, above) are tailored to meet these requirements.

Finally, Article 17 of the Convention contains a guarantee of equal treatment "in respect of any statutory regulation by a public authority concerning wages and working conditions in general".

The United Kingdom has ratified the European Convention on Establishment. Here too, Turkey is the only non-EEA contracting state. We recommend a review of British law and policy to ensure compliance with the Convention's requirements.

3.4 European Social Charter 1961 and 1996

The 1961 European Social Charter, and its revised version of 1996, are general instruments defining economic and social rights. In each version, Articles 18 and 19 are specifically concerned with migrant workers moving between contracting states.

Article 18 is concerned with protecting "the right to engage in a gainful occupation" – in effect, the right to work. Contracting parties undertake the following as regards inward migration:

- "to apply existing regulations in a spirit of liberality"
- "to simplify existing formalities and to reduce or abolish chancery dues and other charges payable by foreign workers or their employers"
- "to liberalise... regulations governing the employment of foreign workers."

Article 19 of the Social Charter sets out a series of rights for migrant workers. Article 19(1) requires States to maintain – or to satisfy themselves that there are maintained – adequate and free services to assist migrant workers, particularly in obtaining accurate information in relation to their rights and to the conditions of their work permit. States are further required to take all appropriate steps within the limits of the national law to ensure that misleading propaganda relating to immigration and emigration is prohibited.

In accordance with Article 19(2), contracting states are required to adopt appropriate measures in their own jurisdictions to facilitate the departure, journey and reception of migrant workers and their families – and to provide appropriate services for health, medical attention and good hygienic conditions during the journey.

Articles 19(4), (5) and (7) require States to secure to migrant workers lawfully within their territories treatment not less favourable than that of their own nationals, including in respect of the following:

- Remuneration and other employment and working conditions
- Membership of trade unions and enjoyment of the benefits of collective bargaining
- Accommodation
- Employment taxes, dues or contributions payable in respect of employed persons
- Legal proceedings relating to matters referred to in Article 19.

Rights as regards immigration are also recognised. With regard to family reunification, Article 19(6) requires contracting states to "Facilitate as far as possible the reunion of the family of a foreign worker permitted to establish himself in the territory". Article 19(8) requires contracting states parties to ensure that migrant workers lawfully residing within their territories are not expelled unless they endanger national security or offend against public interest or morality.

Under Article 19(9), States party to the Charter are required to permit, within legal limits, the transfer of such parts of the earnings and savings of migrant workers as the migrant workers may desire.

Finally, there are two provisions for language teaching in the 1996 revised Social Charter, although not in the 1961 version. Article 19(11) requires states to "promote and facilitate" the teaching to migrant workers and their families of the national language (or one of them), while Article 19(12) requires states "to promote and facilitate, as far as practicable, the teaching of the migrant worker's mother tongue to the children of the migrant worker".

The United Kingdom has ratified the 1961 Social Charter, although not the 1996 version. It is therefore bound by the 1961 version as regards the following non-EEA states: Croatia, Macedonia and Turkey (who have ratified the 1961 version) and Albania, Andorra, Armenia, Azerbaijan, Bulgaria, Moldova and Romania (who have ratified the 1996 version). Here too, we recommend a review of British practice to ensure compliance with the principles set out in the Social Charter.

3.5 European Convention on the Legal Status of Migrant Workers 1977

The 1977 Convention on Migrant Workers develops on the principles set out in other Council of Europe instruments. Article 8(1) contains a novel proposition by comparison with the earlier instruments, that a work permit "may not as a rule bind the worker to the same employer or the same locality for a period longer than one year". This is plainly a more liberal regime than operates for most categories of migrant in the United Kingdom (see chapter three, above).

The Convention goes further as regards immigration entitlements than the previous instruments. Article 9(4) sets out the principle that a worker who is "temporarily incapable of work" because of illness, accident or involuntary unemployment should be allowed to remain in the territory of a state for at least five months, provided they are eligible for unemployment assistance. Rights of family reunion are conferred by Article 12: they cover the spouse and unmarried children, subject to a possible qualification period of 12 months, and the imposition of resource requirements.

The Convention contains a list of matters in respect of which equal treatment with national workers is required. These include housing (Article 13), education and training (Article 14), social security (Article 18), social and medical assistance (Article 19) and taxation (Article 23). The requirement of equality as regards employment conditions, set out in Article 16(1), extends beyond legal rights to cover equal treatment by all of "legislative or administrative provisions, collective labour agreement or custom". It is moreover supported by the statement in Article 16(2) that the right to equality in employment conditions cannot be the subject of derogation in individual contracts.

The United Kingdom has not ratified the 1977 Convention. To date, eight states have done so, all of whom are EEA members: France, Italy, the Netherlands, Norway, Portugal, Spain, Sweden and Turkey. We recommend that Britain ratify the Convention as a key instrument protecting the rights of migrant workers. In any event, we recommend that it review it policies for compatibility with the Convention, and modify those policies accordingly.

4 The United Nations Migrant Workers Convention

The International Convention on the Protection of the Rights of All Migrant Workers and Members of their Families was negotiated under the aegis of the United Nations, and signed in 1990. It came into force on 1 July 2003, and is now the leading statement of international standards on the treatment of migrant workers.

Part III of the Convention is concerned with the "human rights of all migrant workers and members of their families". Much of it is concerned with the articulation of fundamental rights which are recognised under existing international human rights instruments. There is a list of civil and political rights, including the right to life (Article 9), freedom of religion (Article 12), freedom of expression (Article 13), the right to privacy and family life (Article 14), the right to liberty and security of the person (Article 16), and protection against collective expulsion (Article 22). Of particular relevance to this report are the protection against slavery and forced or compulsory labour in Article 11, and the express statement in Article 21 that it should be "unlawful for anyone, other than a public official duly authorized by law, to confiscate, destroy or attempt to destroy identity documents, documents authorizing entry to or stay, residence or establishment in the national territory or work permits".

Part III also covers fundamental social rights. In the employment context, Article 25(1) provides that migrant workers shall enjoy equal treatment with nationals of the State in respect of "conditions of work", defined to mean remuneration, overtime, hours of work, weekly rest, holidays with pay, safety, health, termination of the employment relationship, as well as "any other conditions of work which, according to national law and practice, are covered by this term". It also requires equality in respect of "other terms of employment", including minimum age of employment, restrictions on home work and "any other matters which, according to national law and practice, are considered a term of employment". Article 25(2) then states expressly that it should not be permissible to derogate by contract from that guarantee of equality of treatment. Article 26 provides that migrant workers should have the right to take part in, join and seek the assistance of trade unions. Recognition is also given to rights of equal treatment as regards social security (Article 27), urgent medical care (Article 28) and public education (Article 30).

Crucially, all of the rights in Part III apply irrespective of whether the migrant workers in question have authorised status or not. There are in addition three provisions which expressly protect the position of unauthorised workers. Of particular significance here is Article 25(3), which provides for the application of employment law to such workers:

"States Parties shall take all appropriate measures to ensure that migrant workers are not deprived of any rights derived from this principle by reason of any irregularity in their stay or employment. In particular, employers shall not be relieved of any legal or contractual obligations, nor shall their obligations be limited in any manner by reason of such irregularity."

Article 28 expressly states that urgent medical care "shall not be refused... by reason of any irregularity with regard to stay or employment". Article 30 provides that the right to schooling of children of migrant workers "shall not be refused or limited by reason of the irregular situation with respect to stay or employment of either parent or by reason of the irregularity of the child's stay..."

The Convention also makes provision for the regularisation of unauthorised persons or workers. On the one hand, Article 35 indicates that there is no right to be regularised: "Nothing in the present part of the Convention shall be interpreted as implying the regularisation of the situation of migrant workers or members of their families who are non-documented or in an irregular situation or any right to such regularization of their situation." That must however be read together with Article 69(1) of the Convention, according to which "States Parties shall, when there are migrant workers and members of their families within their territory in an irregular situation, take appropriate measures to ensure that such a situation does not persist". In practice, this second provision implies the possibility of regularisation of such workers, if they are not to be returned to their states of origin.

The rights in Part IV of the Convention are by contrast confined to migrant workers in a regular situation. Among the general rights conferred upon them are liberty of movement within the territory (Article 39) and the right to participate in public affairs (Article 41). Rights of equal treatment are more extensive in their case, and cover the following: educational institutions, vocational guidance, vocational training, housing, social and health services (all in Article 43), protection against dismissal, unemployment benefits and access to public work schemes (all in Article 54). The right of family reunion is recognised by Articles 44 and 50. It is provided by Article 52 that regular workers should have a free choice of employment after not more than two years.

The Convention therefore contains a range of important and progressive measures that would make a real difference to the lives of many migrant workers. As of June 2005, the Convention had been ratified by 30 countries, although not as yet by any of the major developed receiving countries for migrants.[1] The ratification of the Convention by the United Kingdom would be a major step forward to the wider acceptance and implementation of this important set of rules by the countries where they matter most. The United Kingdom would be seen to be taking a positive lead in promoting the acceptance of migrant workers rights to be treated in a fair and equitable manner. We therefore recommend that the United Kingdom should seek to ratify the Convention as soon as possible. We also recommend a formal review of current immigration rules and policies in the light of the obligations set out in the Convention.

5 Unauthorised workers and international law

As we have seen, one of the significant features of the Migrant Workers Convention is its recognition that all workers, including those lacking immigration authorisation, should be able to uphold employment law. It can be argued that there are certain labour rights which are of a status equivalent to fundamental human rights – including at least the 'core labour standards' contained within the ILO's Declaration of Fundamental Rights and Principles at Work issued in 1998. These rights are the right not to be discriminated against, the right to freedom of association and collective bargaining, and the right not to be subjected to child labour or to forced labour. It can also be argued that the principle of non-discrimination in international law must mean that where two individuals are working in comparable situations, they should be afforded the same protections, and not be discriminated against on an arbitrary ground such as immigration status.

This line of reasoning was given substantial support by the Inter-American Court of Human Rights in its Advisory Opinion OC-18/03, delivered on 17 September 2003.[2] The advisory opinion was requested in the wake of the United States Supreme Court's controversial decision in March 2002 in *Hoffman Plastic Compounds Inc v National Labor Relations Board*, that an undocumented migrant worker illegally fired from his job for union organising was not entitled to compensation for lost wages.[3] In May of that year, the government of Mexico requested an advisory opinion from the Inter-American Court, asking whether such practices violated international human rights laws. Several other countries in the region – although not the United States – filed briefs in the case.

The Advisory Opinion broadly held that undocumented workers are entitled not to be discriminated against in the protection given by labour rights, including freedom of association, wages, protection from discrimination, health and safety protections and back pay, as to citizens and those working lawfully in a country. The Court said that,

"the migratory status of a person can never be a justification for depriving him of the enjoyment and exercise of his human rights, including those related to employment. On assuming an employment relationship, the migrant acquires rights as a worker, which must be recognised and guaranteed, irrespective of his regular or irregular status in the State of employment. These rights are a consequence of the employment relationship."[4]

Drawing on the core labour standards contained in the ILO's Declaration of Fundamental Principles and Rights at Work, the Court specifically listed many employment rights which ought to be guaranteed to migrant workers, regardless of their immigration status:

"In the case of migrant workers, there are certain rights that assume a fundamental importance and yet are frequently violated, such as: the prohibition of obligatory or forced labour; the prohibition and abolition of child labour; special care for women workers, and the rights corresponding to: freedom of association and to organise and join a trade union, collective negotiation, fair wages for work performed, social security, judicial and administrative guarantees, a working day of reasonable length with adequate working conditions (safety and health), rest and compensation."[5]

The Advisory Opinion of the Inter-American Court of Human Rights was followed in November 2003 by a decision of the ILO Committee on Freedom of Association, on a complaint by the AFL-CIO of the United States and the *Confederación de Trabajadores de México*.[6] The

Committee on Freedom of Association expressed the view that the US Supreme Court's decision in the *Hoffman* case violated the ILO core principles on freedom of association, since "the remedial measures left to the NLRB in cases of illegal dismissals of undocumented workers are inadequate to ensure effective protection against acts of anti-union discrimination".[7] The Committee recommended action to bring US law "into conformity with freedom of association principles... with the aim of ensuring effective protection for all workers against acts of anti-union discrimination in the wake of the Hoffman decision".[8]

What is revealed by these decisions of the Inter-American Court of Human Rights and the ILO Committee on Freedom of Association, together with Article 25 of the UN Migrant Workers Convention, is that there is growing international support for the principle that unauthorised migrant workers should not be excluded from the protection of employment law. That is also the position which we have taken in this report (see chapter five). In the light of those international developments, we recommend that British law be amended to end the application of the doctrine of illegality to unauthorised migrant workers.

6 Conclusion

This chapter has sought to document the principal international instruments which relate to the position of migrant workers, in response to their usual omission from policy debates on labour migration in the United Kingdom. Many of the relevant international agreements are already binding upon the United Kingdom: ILO Convention 97, the Convention on Social and Medical Assistance, the Convention on Establishment, and the European Social Charter. In those cases, we recommend a formal review of policy to ensure compliance with them. In the case of the European Convention on Migrant Workers and the UN Migrant Workers Convention, meanwhile, we recommend both ratification and, in the interim, a formal review of the compatibility of British policy with their provisions, to be followed by the modification of policy to bring it into line with international standards.

In the context of this report as a whole, what is striking is the extent to which these international texts elaborate a rights-based approach to labour migration. The implications of these instruments for British policy are often close to recommendations for reform which have been made in previous chapters. The many points of overlap include the principle of respect for the right to work, recognition of a right to change employer, equal treatment in social assistance, rights of family reunion, the enforcement of employment rights by unauthorised workers, and the unacceptability of prolonged situations of unauthorised work. The call to uphold international norms in relation to labour migration should not therefore be seen as an abstract one: it is a further argument for placing the rights of workers at the heart of labour migration policy.

Notes

1 The states which had ratified the Convention by 29 June 2005 were: Algeria, Azerbaijan, Belize, Bolivia, Bosnia and Herzegovina, Burkina Faso, Cape Verde, Chile, Colombia, Ecuador, Egypt, El Salvador, Ghana, Guatemala, Guinea, Kyrgyzstan, Libya, Mali, Mexico, Morocco, Philippines, Senegal, Seychelles, Sri Lanka, Syria, Tajikistan, Timor-Leste, Turkey, Uganda and Uruguay.
2 The text of the Advisory Opinion can be found at: http://www.corteidh.or.cr/serieapdf_ing/seriea_18_ing.pdf.
3 535 US 137 (2002).
4 Advisory Opinion OC-18/03, para 134.
5 Ibid, para 157.
6 ILO Committee on Freedom of Association, Case No. 2227, Report No. 332, Complaints against the Government of the United States presented by the American Federation of Labor and the Congress of Industrial Organizations (AFL-CIO) and the Confederation of Mexican Workers (CTM), 2003.
7 Ibid, para 610.
8 Ibid, para 611.

Chapter 7

Summary of main recommendations

Chapter 3: Legal migration

Entitlement to work (section 3)

● The Workers' Registration Scheme for A8 nationals should be brought to an end as soon as possible. If the Workers' Registration Scheme is to be maintained, the 12-month exception should apply from one year after a worker starts employment and should not require continuous employment.

● Bulgarian and Romanian nationals should be entitled to treatment parallel to that given to A8 nationals. They should either be subject to procedural restrictions for the same transitional period as A8 nationals, or have restrictions upon them removed at the same time as A8 nationals.

● Britain should opt in to the Long-term Residents Directive (Directive 2003/109). This would allow movement between Britain and other Member States for employment by long-term residents who are from third countries.

Skilled employment (section 4)

● The skills threshold within the work permit system should be removed. The current minimum requirement is a university degree, HND qualification, or three years' experience of working at NVQ Level 3 or above.

● In 'shortage occupations', workers ought either to be permitted to take any job in that occupation, or else be allowed unrestricted labour market access.

● Restrictions on switching into work permit employment should be removed. This is particularly important in the case of switching from permit-free employment and from labour migration schemes.

- The requirement that work permit workers receive comparable treatment with other employees ought to be enforceable by the worker. This should be done by making discrimination by employers on grounds of immigration status a breach of the Race Relations Act.

Less skilled employment (section 5)

- It is necessary to elaborate a general framework for less-skilled labour migration, applicable to all sectors, and not limited by quotas.
- Transparent mechanisms should be established for the recruitment of workers to labour migration schemes, which should be based as far as possible in the United Kingdom.
- Workers on labour migration schemes should be permitted to stay on with their current employers after the initial period of employment permission has expired.
- Workers on labour migration schemes ought to be permitted to bring their spouse and children with them.

Working holidaymakers (section 6)

- Places on the working holidaymaker scheme should be allocated by means of an annual quota per state or region.
- Access to the working holidaymaker scheme should not be limited to nationals of states with return arrangements with the United Kingdom.

Horizontal issues (section 7)

- Migrant workers should have an unlimited right to change employer and occupation after a short period, such as three months, has elapsed. Workers on labour migration schemes should have a right to change employer without a qualifying period.
- EEA nationals should have access to social benefits while looking for work in the United Kingdom. A8 nationals should not be excluded from non-contributory benefits after employment in the United Kingdom. Migrant workers from outside the EEA should also be eligible for non-contributory benefits when they cease employment.
- An application for settlement should depend upon proof that an individual is in employment at the end of the four-year period. It should not be necessary for an employer to certify that this is the case.
- The period of employment after which settlement can be obtained should not be increased to five years, and those in permit-free employment should not be excluded from the possibility of settlement.

- Charges for immigration documents linked to employment should be set at a low level, so as not to deter migration, and so as to reflect the obligatory nature of the immigration control process.
- If employment authorisation and immigration permission are to be dealt with together, that should be done centrally, rather than through the entry clearance process.
- There should be effective rights of appeal against the refusal of authorisation for employment or of a related immigration permission.

Chapter 4: Unauthorised working

Regularisation (section 6)

- The United Kingdom should implement a collective regularisation programme for unauthorised persons. Regularisation should be based on proof of presence rather than on proof of employment.
- The programme should operate on the basis of 'earned regularisation'. Applicants would first obtain temporary residence and work permission. They would be eligible for permanent residence on completion of a temporary residence period, which should be the same as the period of work permit employment needed for settlement. It should also be necessary to show stable formal sector employment at the end of the period.

Asylum seekers (section 7)

- All asylum seekers should be granted permission to work if they are still waiting for an initial decision, or are still in the asylum appeals system, six months after the date of their initial asylum application. There should be discretion to grant permission to work within a shorter time scale.
- Permission to work for asylum seekers should extend to self-employment and business activities.
- Asylum seekers who have exhausted their appeals, but who cannot be returned to their states of origin, should be granted a temporary status which permits employment.
- Section 10 of the Asylum and Immigration (Treatment of Claimants, etc) Act 2004, which allows the provision of accommodation to non-returnable asylum seekers to be made conditional on community service, should be repealed.

Immigration control in the workplace (section 8)

- The provision for employer checks and penalties based upon section 8 of the Asylum and Immigration Act 1996 should be repealed.

The current proposals for an 'on the spot' civil penalty, and for a strengthened criminal offence of knowingly employing an unauthorised worker, should not be proceeded with.

- Identity cards should not be used to check immigration status at the workplace.

Trafficking for exploitation (section 9)

- The United Kingdom should agree to Council Directive 2004/81 on the issuing of residence permits to third country nationals who are the victims of all forms of trafficking in human beings.

- The current shelter scheme for victims of trafficking should be expanded, and should include victims of people trafficking other than for sexual exploitation.

Chapter 5: Migrant workers and employment law

Unauthorised workers and labour law (section 2.1)

- Unauthorised workers should not be prevented by the doctrine of illegality from enforcing employment contracts and employment rights. This protection should cover both the breach of immigration laws and the non-payment of taxes and national insurance contributions.

Gangmasters and agencies (section 2.2)

- The Gangmasters' Licensing Authority should not be merged with the Health and Safety Executive. Its focus should be on the enforcement of labour standards, and its role should not extend to immigration enforcement.

- The licensing of agencies and intermediaries should be extended to all sectors, and not be confined to gangmasters in agriculture, shell fishing and related processing sectors.

- An intermediary and a user undertaking should be jointly liable, as employers, for compliance with the employment rights of their workers.

- The principle that workers should not have to pay intermediaries should be re-affirmed. It should be stated in legislation that any contract or arrangement for the payment of such fees is unenforceable within the United Kingdom. It should also be expressly provided that the rules against charging by United Kingdom employment agencies extend to requests for such payments made outside the United Kingdom.

The coverage of employment law (section 2.3)

- The Government should use the power in section 23 of the Employment Relations Act 1999 to extend all employment rights to 'workers' other than employees.
- There should be no service qualification for core employment rights.

Discrimination law (section 3.1)

- The Race Relations Act should be amended to include immigration status as a prohibited ground of discrimination, both in the employment sphere and beyond it.
- The rule against harassment introduced into the Race Relations Act in 2003 should be applied to discrimination on grounds of nationality, and also to discrimination on grounds of immigration status.
- Some forms of conduct towards migrant workers ought to be automatically classified as breaches of the rule against immigration status discrimination, including the following: failure to provide a statement of terms and conditions, failure to provide an itemised pay statement, failure to pay the minimum wage, the making of unauthorised deductions from wages, and the denial of trade union rights.

Terms of employment (sections 3.2 and 3.3)

- The written statement of contract terms provided for in section 1 of the Employment Rights Act 1996 should be provided in the migrant worker's own language or in a language in which the migrant worker is literate.
- The statement of contract terms should be provided to all workers either within one week, or by the first pay date, whichever is later. Failure to provide the statement should give rise to a right to compensation for workers.

Payments and deductions (sections 3.4 to 3.6)

- Failure to provide an itemised pay statement, as required by section 8 of the Employment Rights Act 1996, should give rise to a right to compensation for workers.
- The sanctions for non-compliance with the national minimum wage should be strengthened. There should be a penalty element in all cases of non-compliance, and all penalties should be payable to the workers in question.
- A new 'Truck Act' to regulate both the payment of wages and deductions should be introduced. It should be unlawful for employers to provide goods and services as an alternative to wages, and for

employers to make deductions from wages for goods and services provided. It should be unlawful for an employer to make deductions from pay, other than for accommodation, where the effect would be to reduce the worker's gross earnings to less than the national minimum wage.

• The 'accommodation offset' in the minimum wage legislation, which currently allows a maximum deduction of £3.75 per day, should apply in all cases. Employers should not be permitted to make any deduction for accommodation within which individuals do not have their own room.

Working time (section 3.7)

• An individual opt-out from the 48 hour maximum working week should not be valid unless it is attached to a document in the worker's mother tongue, or a language in which the worker is literate, which informs the worker of the right to opt into the 48 hour week without penalty.

• Legislation on parental leave, time off in a family emergency, and requests for flexible working to care for children should be clarified to ensure that these rights relate to children outside the United Kingdom.

Health and safety (section 3.8)

• Employers should be under an express duty to allow for the particular circumstances of migrant workers when fulfilling their health and safety obligations.

• There should be a statutory duty on employers who hire workers whose mother tongue is not English to communicate health and safety information in a language in which the workers are literate.

• Employers should be required to monitor and report separately to the Health and Safety Executive on the size of their migrant workforce, and on health and safety issues relevant to them. The Health and Safety Executive should have a duty to inspect workplaces with significant numbers of migrant workers at regular intervals (such as six months).

Dismissals and other employer decisions (section 3.9)

• Employers should be obliged to provide copies of contractual grievance procedures or the statutory grievance procedure to workers in a language in which the workers are literate.

• The statutory requirement that dismissal, disciplinary and grievance procedures be conducted in a manner that enables employees to explain their case should be clarified, so as to entitle a worker who is not fluent in English to an interpreter and translation.

- An employee who has been dismissed because the employer believes their employment is unauthorised should have a period of three months prior to a dismissal's coming into force, in order for them to clarify or regularise their position.
- It should be automatically unfair to dismiss a migrant worker who raises a grievance with an employer, beyond the assertion of a statutory right.
- Migrant workers who make legitimate complaints about employer treatment should be immune from immigration enforcement, should be free to take alternative employment, and should be entitled to claim social benefits.

Trade union rights (section 3.10)

- Where a migrant worker is victimised by an employer for having joined or taken part in a trade union or industrial action, this should be treated as a breach of the law on discrimination on grounds of immigration status.
- Trade unions should have autonomous rights within labour law, including rights of access to a workforce with a view to recruitment, and the right to enforce employment laws independently of individual workers.

Changes of employer (section 3.11)

- It should be a criminal offence for an employer, agency or other body to retain a worker's identity documents without their consent. It should also be a criminal offence for any employer to require a bond from an employee against future performance or employment.

Social security (section 3.12)

- There should be a legal obligation on an employer to inform migrant workers, in their mother tongue, or in a language in which the workers are literate, of the existence of statutory sick pay and statutory maternity pay, and of how to claim them.

Information about employment rights (section 3.13)

- All migrant workers who register with the immigration authorities should receive information, both in English and in their own language, as to their legal entitlements. This information should be prepared in co-operation with the TUC.
- The main public bodies concerned with employment law, including the Employment Tribunal Service, the Health and Safety Executive and ACAS, should endeavour to provide information in the major languages of migrant workers. These bodies should also have a duty to ensure that, where migrant workers lack fluency in English, they should be able to proceed with a complaint in their own language.

Chapter 6: International agreements on migrant workers

ILO standards (section 2)

● The United Kingdom should formally review its policies to ensure it respects the protections for migrant workers set out in the Migration for Employment Convention (ILO Convention 97) and in the Migrant Workers (Supplementary Provisions) Convention (ILO Convention 143).

● The United Kingdom should also review the compatibility of its policies with the standards set out in the Migration for Employment Recommendation (ILO Recommendation 86) and the Migrant Workers Recommendation (ILO Recommendation 151) and make any necessary changes.

Council of Europe standards (section 3)

● The United Kingdom should ratify Protocol 12 to the European Convention on Human Rights.

● The United Kingdom should ratify the European Convention on the Legal Status of Migrant Workers of 1977.

● The United Kingdom should formally review the compatibility of its policies with the protections for migrant workers set out in the relevant Council of Europe treaties and make any necessary changes. These are the European Convention on Social and Medical Assistance, the European Convention on Establishment, the European Social Charter and the European Convention on the Legal Status of Migrant Workers.

United Nations standards (section 4)

● The United Kingdom should ratify the International Convention on the Protection of the Rights of All Migrant Workers and Members of their Families of 1990. It should also formally review the compatibility of its policies with the standards set out in the Convention and make any necessary changes.

Unauthorised workers (section 5)

● The United Kingdom should give effect to the international human rights principle that unauthorised workers should be able to enforce employment laws.

Chapter 7 : **Summary of main recommendations**